Just Try It!

FFCworks...

HEALING LIFE'S HURTS

FIVE FOLD CYCLE

Method of Healing Personal Hurt

Workbook

KENNETH L. FABBI

Kenneth L Fabbi Publication
Lethbridge, Alberta, T1K 7T9, CANADA
FiveFoldCycle@gmail.com

FIVE FOLD CYCLE – METHOD OF HEALING PERSONAL HURT
Copyright © 2016 by Kenneth L. Fabbi
First Printing — 1990
Second Printing — 2016
Third Printing — 2019
WORKBOOK — 2024
First Printing — 2023

All rights reserved.

Unless otherwise indicated, all biblical quotations are taken from the New Revised Standard Version Bible, copyright © 1989 the Division of Christian Education of the National Council of the Churches of Christ in the United States of America. Used by permission. All rights reserved.

No part of this publication may be reproduced in any form, or by any means, electronic or mechanical, including photocopying, recording, or any information browsing, storage, or retrieval system, without permission in writing from the Author.

Kenneth, the author, would welcome your communication at FiveFoldCycle@gmail.com .

ISBN:
Paperback: 978-1-7771066-3-8

Subjects: *Healing Prayer - - Christianity - -*
               Problem Solving - - Growth

I. Title   II. Fabbi, Kenneth L.

TABLE OF CONTENTS

Preface	vii
Introduction	1
Five Fold Cycle – Diagram	3

I. **An Understanding of the Background** — 5

    1. We are all Broken People — 5
    Study Notes: What do you learn from each Scripture?
    Workshop # 1 - How Were You Bruised?
    Prayer: Lord Transform Me
    The Weaver

    2. What do we do to Break out of This Cycle? — 8
    The Exchange
    A Few Aspects of this Exchange
    Study Notes: The Exchange

    3. Why do we not have Perfect Order? — 12
    Scripture Encounter – In Adam or In Christ

    4. We Have Free Will and Choice — 14
    Choice Line
    Scripture Encounter – Examples of Free Choice in the Bible
    Study Notes: Not My Will but Yours Be Done
    Prayer: Lord, I give you freedom to work within me
    Workshop # 2 - Proclamation: in Free Choice we accept Jesus
                           as Lord of our life.

    5. The Separation of Body, Mind, Soul, and Spirit — 19
    The Body
        Scripture Encounter – Our Temple
        Workshop # 3 – Targeting Our Body Points
    The Mind — 21
    The Soul
        Workshop # 4 – Forgiveness
        Prayer: For Forgiving Heart
    The Spirit — 24
        Study Notes: Collaborate with Holy Spirit
        Scripture Encounter – Availability of the Holy Spirit
        Prayer: For the Baptism in the Spirit
    The Web Theory — 28
    Workshop # 5 – Envision yourself in Heaven.
    Scripture Encounter – New and Radical Change
    Workshop # 6 – Get rid of Old Habits.

    Scripture Encounter – Body is the Temple of the Holy Spirit: 32
    Diagram – Four Basic Components Explained
    Study Notes: We are Spirit First

6. Choices   34
Workshop # 7 – Identity in Christ Jesus
Scripture Encounter - Adoption
Prayer: For Adoption

7. So Let's Review   39
A Pie
Spiritual Law – Negatives Are Not Under Jesus' Rule
Workshop # 8 – Fruit of the Spirit
Spiritual Law – God Uses All Things
Christ Before Thy Door Is Waiting – by W. Rainey, circa 1883.

II. Process   44

Step One: Becoming God Focused   44
    Scripture Encounter – Asking and Receiving
    Workshop # 9 – Becoming God Focused

Step Two: Identify a Problem or Issue   47

    a) Identify   47
    Wedge
    Nibbling Theory

    b) Sources   49
    Plaster Theory
    Bitter Root
    Workshop # 10 – Negative Vows or Negative Self-Talk   51

    c) Gifts of the Holy Spirit   52
    Cube Theory
    Scripture Encounter – Roles of the Holy Spirit

    d) Problems are Inter-Connected   54
    Water Glass and Cube Theory

Step Three: Cleaning   55

    a) It's Simple (As All Things of God)   55
    Scripture Encounter – There is no Middle Ground
    Choice Line - Reworked
    The Art of Forgiveness
    Spiritual Law – What You Focus On is What You Get
    Spiritual Law - Don't Hold On To Your Hurts

Scripture Encounter – Understanding Forgiveness
Prayer: Forgiveness Prayer

    b) **Don't Dwell** — 63

    c) **Spirits And Bondage** — 64

    d) **Thoughts Cause Feelings** — 64
        Theory Of Nibbling The Cube
        Spiritual Law - Problems Will Not Be Beyond Your Strength.

Step Four: Filling — 68

    a) **It's Time To Fill** — 68
        Let's Review
        Study Notes: What Does God Call You?
        Scripture Encounter – Power of Attorney

    b) **Don't Forget The Others.** — 72

    c) **Asking.** — 72
        Study Notes: Abraham's Faith

    d) **Warning.** — 73
        Scripture Encounter – Warnings

    e) **You And I Leak** — 75
        Human Sieve

Step Five: Thank the Lord — 77

Recapitulation — 78

III. Instructions — 79

    1. **When do you use This Method?** — 79
        Negatives to Positives Through the Cross
        Workshop # 12 – Healing Negative Thoughts

    2. **Let's Look at Depression** — 82

        Diagram – Anger, Guilt and Depression — 82

        a) *Anger (Unforgiveness)* — 82

        b) *Guilt* — 83
        c) *Depression* — 83
            Five Fold Cycle Process Is Simple

IV.	**Personal Care Planning**	84
	Root Problem	
	Bondage	
	Ministry	
	Personal Care Plan	

My Prayer — 87

NOTES: — 89

Appendix 'A' - Five Fold Cycle – Method of Healing Personal Hurt — 91

Appendix 'B' - The Holy Spirit and the Gifts of the Holy Spirit — 93
    Understanding The Gifts

Appendix 'C' - Every Negative Becomes a Positive in the Cross — 96

Appendix 'D' - Supplemental Readings — 97

    1) *Inner Healing References*
    2) *Gifts of the Holy Spirit References*
    3) *Deliverance References*
    4) *Research Review of Interaction of Religion and Health*

Appendix 'E' - Scripture as Medicine: The Rx from the Doctor Jesus — 99

Appendix 'F' – Prayer for Salvation — 103

Appendix 'G' – Receiving the Holy Spirit – Baptism in the Holy Spirit — 104
    Prayer for The Baptism in The Spirit
    God's Temple is in You – Meditation — 106

Appendix 'H' – Who Am I In Christ? / *Identity* — 107

Appendix 'I' – I Am in Christ Therefore … / *Your Position in Christ* — 109

Appendix 'J' – Practical Steps to Forgiveness — 112

Appendix 'K' – Intercessory Prayers — 113
    Scriptural Arguments for Intercessors

Appendix 'L' – Healing Through Communion — 115

Answers To Study Notes — 120

FAQ – Questions offer a deeper understanding: — 127

Preface

When I was beginning my work as a Christian counsellor, I wondered how I would teach people about the wonders of our Lord's healing. I had read many books by people involved in the Christian Healing field, but none seemed to tell people how to do it. They all said things like: "come to the Lord in prayer", "let the Lord take your suffering", "offer it up to the Lord", "give it to the Lord", but no one told you how do to that. I was amazed at all the good ideas and prayerful, holy people; everyone seemed to know that the Lord would fix things, but how?

As I prayed and counselled people, I found that the Lord was showing me simple things regarding prayer, such as images, theories, truths, and methods. All of the knowledge came together as wisdom. In prayer I offered the ideas to very hurting people and the Lord healed them. The miraculous incidents overshadowed the everyday events. Each day it continued to amaze me; some of the miracles were just teasers to encourage us on.

The Bible is littered with things that are impossible; we call them miracles.

I remember one day when Carol had come by for some prayer; she was worried and depressed that day. When she left, I went back to writing at my desk. I then heard this grinding coming from some car outside. Over and over I heard someone trying to start their car, and the starter ground and ground. Finally, it had bothered me enough that I poked my head out, only to find Carol still parked in front of the building. I went over and looked through the open passenger window. "Not starting?" I asked. "Let's say a prayer". Carol was always open to prayer. We said a quick prayer, then she tried the starter again and it started with no trouble. I smiled with amazement. The Lord had encouraged us – it was just a little teaser from the Lord to reassure us that He was around and active.

I became more and more convinced of the power of healing prayer as time went on; the Lord was healing my personal hurts and He was using me to teach others to receive Healing.

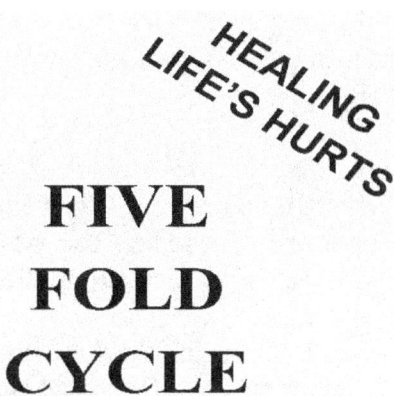

HEALING LIFE'S HURTS

FIVE FOLD CYCLE

Method of Healing Personal Hurt

Miraculous incidents overshadowed the everyday events.

The Bible is littered with things that are impossible – we call them miracles.

Just Try It!

FFC works...

I started to collect my ideas and put them into a methodology; it was so simple that people didn't believe it would work. I found myself saying hundreds of times, "*Just Try It!* Experiment!" Generally, I could get the clients to try it as an experiment. We would do it in my office with the problems they presented to me, and I would challenge them to try it at home. When they came back the next time, I would ask how they did, and the majority of the time they said that they had found more peace.

Writing the Method so that people could take it home and put it into their theoretical perspective, came next. It helped me get organized and see the inter-activeness of the steps. I thank people like my brother Ron, Maria Lemire, Ron Favreau, and the many clients and friends who taught me and challenged me along the way.

I also thank the Lord, because I know it wasn't me who put this all together. The Lord caused me to teach; He shared His Holy Spirit and the Gifts, and He helped me become systematic. When He set me out to minister to others, I was anything but organized. I was inconsistent, lived a sinful life, and was going nowhere with lots of speed. Today I feel at peace and directed. This comes from the Lord.

I offer the following material to you. I wish and pray that you might find it useful. I ask you to *Just Try It* out. I ask you to share it with anyone under the Lord's direction. Remember, I am not the Healer, and you are not the Healer. Jesus is the Healer.

You will find that this method is simple, as are all things of the Lord – it will fit into your spiritual life. The Lord will guide you in making it fruitful as long as you listen to Him. Be open to how the Lord wants to deal with you. He deals with each one of us in a personal and private way.

It is interesting to see that Jesus never related to a crowd, even when there was a flood of people around Him. He always had eyes, ears and heart for each individual in front of Him. He didn't wave his hand over the crowd to perform a mass healing. He reached out and touched one leper. He forgave one sinner. He answered one question. To Jesus the individual was important.

The Creator, God the Father, is an expert in our inner workings. He doesn't need a manual to understand our hearts are 'out of order'. He has a personal solution set aside for each of us. His Love is demonstrative in that He does not overlook our sin but rather saves us from it.

Have fun and enjoy your reading.

– Ken.

_____

Acknowledgements:

The gender, names, locations, professions, ages, and appearances of the persons whose stories are told in this book have been changed to protect their identities, unless they have granted permission to the author or publisher to do otherwise.

A special thanks to Kay Peterson for the original pictures back in 1990 and up-dating some for newer edition. And also, thanks to Gerben Terpstra for his fine drafting of the *Five Fold Cycle* Image and other diagrams. I appreciate you folks.

To my Editor Laura Petker, who helped me in 2016, I want to acknowledge that without your help this material would be very hard to read. Thank you for your professional help!

This Workbook is a collection of workshops and material that I have used over time. Often, I don't really remember who originated the ideas or where they came from. Generally, as I gleaned the material, developed it and played with it, it has become mine. I want to thank the many friends and acquaintances who inspired me and shared their material. I do appreciate you and I pray the Lord is blessing you.

Many thanks to Lisa Feser and Karla Conte who edited this workbook. You folks are a blessing. As well as editing, you interpret my thoughts and inspire very good ideas that develop it and make it flow. I really appreciate your care and your love. Thank you!

Introduction

In this book I outline a *Method of Healing Personal Hurt*[1] entitled *Five Fold Cycle*. It is a systems approach to problem solving and is meant to be used to aid in the healing of memories, healing of emotions, healing of trauma, healing of self-image, healing of relationships, and the other inner healing prayers. It is a method of fine-tuning healing prayer to better utilize the Lord's 'pruning/cleansing'.

Scripture describes the Lord's pruning and cleansing in this manner:

"I am the true vine, and my Father is the vinegrower. He removes every branch in me that bears no fruit. Every branch that bears fruit he prunes to make it bear more fruit."
John 15: 1-2

It is a simple message from the Lord. He says we are to be 'in Him' and then he will 'prune' (cleanse) us.

An old song comes to mind which most adequately describes the process we must use to receive the Lord's cleansing:

> What a friend we have in Jesus
> all our sins and griefs to bear
> What a privilege to carry
> Everything to God in Prayer
>
> Oh what peace we often forfeit
> Oh what needless pains we bear
> All because we do not carry
> Everything to God in prayer

The song describes the process necessary to receive the Lord's cleansing.

The process is simple: we must bring each individual issue or problem to the Lord and ask for his help in cleansing it. As we do this, we join to Him like a branch to a tree and He joins us, giving us nourishment and peace.

"Abide in me as I abide in you. Just as the branch cannot bear fruit by itself unless it abides in the vine, neither can you unless you abide in me."
John 15: 4

We also come to realize that we cannot bear fruit, or as the Alcoholics Anonymous movement says: we are powerless unless we abide in Him.

"I am the vine, you are the branches. Those who abide in me and I in them bear much fruit, because apart from me you can do nothing."
John 15: 5

Let us look at the simplicity of the process God has described for us. I would describe it in this manner:

We come to God in prayer. We focus on an issue or problem, asking for the Lord's help through His Holy Spirit. The Holy Spirit guides us as we take it to the Lord in prayer, asking for cleansing/pruning. After the cleansing we ask the Lord to fill us with His blessings. And finally, we move the focus off of ourselves and refocus on the Lord in thanksgiving and praise.

Five Fold Cycle – Diagram

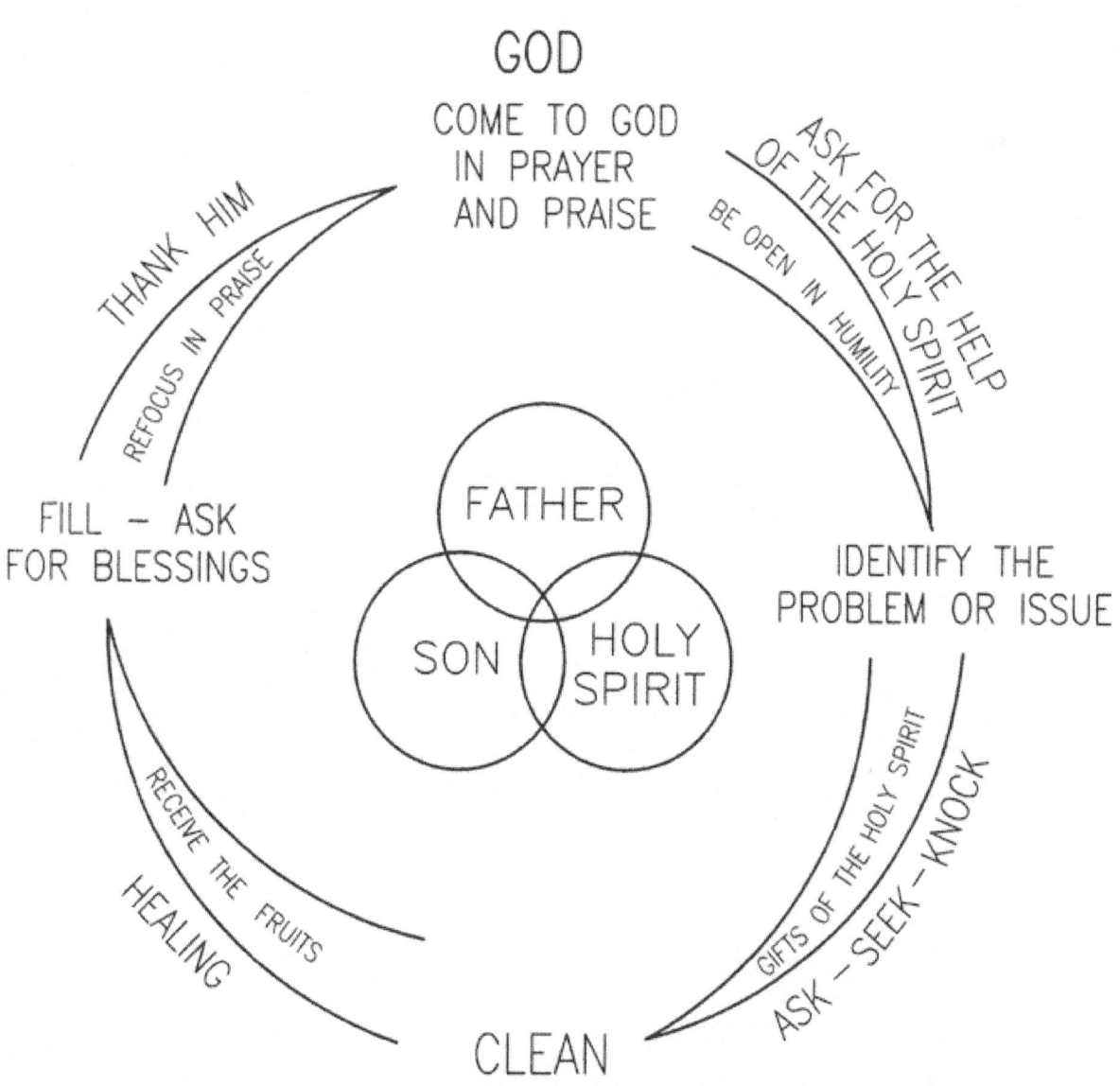

Why do we need inner healing?

Why do we need this process?

To understand these questions, we must look at the scriptural background which leads to the need for this process. Then we will look at the process itself and how *Five Fold Cycle* – a problem solving method – is used.

I. An Understanding of the Background

1. We are all Broken People

It doesn't matter who you are, what family you grew up in, nor your financial circumstances – you have been hurt. We are all broken people!

Look back at your parents for a minute. It is often easier to see their brokenness before we can see our own. Each one of your parents had their problems, their hurts, their wounds. Take your mother for instance. What were her wounds? Did she have mother problems? Was there an absence of a mother, or was she overbearing?

Did you pick up her fears, her anger, her bitterness, or maybe her guilt and lack of self-confidence? Take a moment to pause – close your eyes and reflect on the brokenness you received from your mother.

Look at your father. What were his wounds? How did it affect you? Did you learn pride and confidence, or was it fear and mistrust? Was he sensitive and loving, or a tyrant? Or maybe just ineffective? Take a moment to close your eyes, and reflect on your father and the brokenness you received from him.

We are a product of our broken parents. They experienced hurt throughout their life, and some of that hurt passed on to us.

STUDY NOTES:
WHAT DO YOU LEARN FROM EACH SCRIPTURE?

Exodus 20: 4-5 _____

Exodus 34: 6-7 _____

Leviticus 26: 40-42 _____

Deuteronomy 5: 9-10 _____

Deuteronomy 7: 9-11 _____

Jeremiah 32: 18 _____

We see that iniquity, the sins of the fathers, come down through the generations, as do blessings. We are all broken because we have received brokenness through our family. No family is perfect; we all have wounds. God offers us healing as we attach to Him, as branches do to the vine.

WORKSHOP # 1

- <u>HOW WERE YOU BRUISED?</u>

We might ask the questions: Who are the significant people in your life? And what were the positive and negative influences on your life?

<u>Significant Individual:</u>   <u>Positive Influences:</u>   <u>Negative Influences:</u>

_____   _____   _____

_____   _____   _____

_____   _____   _____

_____   _____   _____

Decision: Give God the right to transformation these negative influences

(Take these issues that bruised you, one by one, through the prayer below. Ask the Lord to transform them by His grace. The positive and negative events are part of our story. God is a redeemer and doesn't erase every scar from our past, but transforms them by His grace and mercy.)

Now don't get me wrong, our parents had good points, too. They loved, cared, and nurtured. They did the best with the things they had to offer. But each one of us was wounded. Each one of us is a broken person.

Prayer:

LORD TRANSFORM ME

Lord, I ask you to transform me. Take the negatives influences _____ that have formed my life and transform them with Your grace and Your mercy…

The Weaver

My life is but a weaving
Between my God and me.
I cannot choose the colors
He weaveth steadily.

Oft' times He weaveth sorrow;
And I in foolish pride
Forget He sees the upper
And I the underside.

Not 'til the loom is silent
And the shuttles cease to fly
Will God unroll the canvas
And reveal the reason why.

The dark threads are as needful
In the weaver's skillful hand
As the threads of gold and silver
In the pattern He has planned

He knows, He loves, He cares;
Nothing this truth can dim.
He gives the very best to those
Who leave the choice to Him.

- Author Unknown

2. What do we do to Break out of This Cycle?

The question comes to mind then: what do we do to break out of this cycle? This is the central question to this book. Through Christ we have been offered a solution to our brokenness:

> This was to fulfill what had been spoken through the prophet Isaiah, "He took our infirmities and bore our diseases."
> Matthew 8: 17

Even back in Isaiah of the Old Testament, it was predicted that Jesus would come and take away our sins and hurts. God is faithful to his promises!

> Surely he has borne our infirmities and carried our diseases; yet we accounted him stricken, struck down by God, and afflicted. But he was wounded for our transgressions, crushed for our iniquities; upon him was the punishment that made us whole, and by his bruises we are healed.
> Isaiah 53: 4-5

THE EXCHANGE

(The Exchange Detail taken from Derek Prince [2])

If you have a need or problem in your life, there is only one place and one place alone where you must go to find the provision or God's solution. And that one place is the Cross of Jesus.

Through what Jesus accomplished by His death on the Cross, every provision of God for you; spiritual, physical, material, for time or eternity has been made available.

There is no other basis than the Cross for all the provision of God.

It is through the Cross and through the Cross only, that you can come to God and receive His provisions and His blessings.

In order to do that, you need to understand the basic nature of what took place when Jesus died on the Cross. At that point *a divinely ordained exchange* took place. Ordained by God and predicted many centuries before in the Prophets of Israel. The Exchange is all summed up in one key verse of the prophet Isaiah 53: 6:

> *All we like sheep have gone astray; we have all turned to our own way, and the LORD has laid on him (and Him is Jesus) the iniquity of us all.*

That is the absolute center of all that God has to offer for us. It is entirely the grace of God. We have no claim upon God, we could not have demanded this from God, but in His infinite grace and mercy God ordained this exchange.

Simply: God laid on Jesus the iniquity of us all. (*Iniquity* could also be translated *rebellion*. Rebellion and all the consequences and judgments that come upon rebellion.)

Our rebellion, the rebellion of the entire sin cursed Adamic race, came upon Jesus upon the Cross, by divine appointment.

That is the negative part of the exchange. The positive side is that in return, all the good that was due to the sinless obedience of Jesus might be available to us. God visited upon Jesus the evil due to us that in return he might make available to us the good due to Jesus.

Simply: The evil came upon Jesus, that the good might be available to us.

Now there is no claim upon God, we could not have demanded this from God but in His infinite grace and mercy God ordained this exchange.

God visited upon Jesus our rebellion and then He endured all the evil consequences of our rebellion which by justice should have come upon us.

The Cross was a divinely ordained exchange.

The evil came upon Jesus, that the good might be offered to us.

A FEW ASPECTS OF THIS EXCHANGE

Jesus was punished that we might be forgiven.

> For the wages of sin is death, but the free gift of God is eternal life in Christ
> Jesus our Lord.
> Romans 6: 23

Jesus bore our sins in His own body on the tree, that we, having died to sins, might live for righteousness.

Jesus was physically wounded that we might be physically healed.

> He himself bore our sins in his body on the cross, so that, free from sins, we
> might live for righteousness; by his wounds you have been healed.
> 1 Peter 2: 24; Isaiah 53: 4 – 6

What Jesus endured physical (wounding with whip, crown of thorns, spit, lance, carrying the cross and hanging on the cross) He did so that we might be physically healed.

Jesus was made sin that we might be made righteous.

> For our sake he made him to be sin who knew no sin, so that in him we might become the righteousness of God.
> 2 Corinthians 5: 21

Jesus was punished that we might be forgiven. He endured the judgment and punishment due to our rebellion, so that in Jesus we become right before God the Father.

Jesus experiences death that we might receive eternal life.

> But we do see Jesus, who for a little while was made lower than the angels, now crowned with glory and honor because of the suffering of death, so that by the grace of God he might taste death for everyone.
> Hebrews 2: 9

What is the exchange? The Exchange is that we might share His Eternal Life. This is redemption.

On the Cross Jesus endured our poverty. He was stripped. He was left totally impoverished. He was left with nothing. He took our poverty that we might share His abundance (2 Corinthians 8: 9).

On the Cross Jesus was rejected by God the Father. He cried out and there came no answer from Heaven. He died of a broken heart, a heart broken by rejection, but by His rejection we have acceptance by God the Father (Matthew 27: 46).

The truth in Scripture is repeated time and time again – evil came on Jesus that the good might be available to us.

Jesus becomes a curse, that we might receive the blessing.

Paul says:

> [13] Christ redeemed us from the curse of the law by becoming a curse for us—for it is written, "Cursed is everyone who hangs on a tree"— [14] in order that in Christ Jesus the blessing of Abraham might come to the Gentiles, so that we might receive the promise of the Spirit through faith.
> Galatians 3: 13-14

This scripture explains this exchange that was foretold in the Deuteronomy 21: 23 of the Old Testament, 'Cursed is everyone who hangs on a tree'.

In the exchange it is obvious: the evil is the curse and the good is the blessing.

The words "bless" or "blessing", occur in the bible approximately 430 times. The word curse in various forms occurs in the bible approximately 160 times.

Jesus had to become a curse that we might be redeemed from the curse and receive the blessing.

STUDY NOTES:
THE EXCHANGE

What was exchanged?

Galatians 3: 13-14 _____

1 Peter 2: 24 _____

Matthew 8: 17 _____

2 Corinthians 5: 21 _____

Hebrews 2: 9 _____

Isaiah 53: 4-6 _____

Deuteronomy 21: 23 _____

Hebrews 9: 15 _____

Hebrews 9: 24-28 _____

Hebrews 10: 10 _____

Romans 6: 23 _____

2 Corinthians 8: 9 _____

Matthew 27: 46 _____

Christ is the mediator of a new covenant – once and for all!
1 Timothy 2: 5

3. Why do we not have Perfect Order?

Biblical history speaks to us of Adam and Eve as being struck in the likeness of God. If we were then cast in the image of God (Genesis 1: 26), then should we not have perfect order? Well yes, but in Genesis Chapter 3 it talks about the fall of Adam and Eve and how this fall has affected all of creation. Basically, we are suffering the effect of their sin. Catholics call this "Original Sin". Paul writes that just like the act 'in Adam' that pulled us down, 'in Jesus' was the act that brought us to life.

> [21] For since death came through a human being, the resurrection of the dead has also come through a human being; [22] for as all die in Adam, so all will be made alive in Christ.
> 1 Corinthians 15: 21-22

With original sin there is a darkness of our intellect, a weakness of our will, and an inclination to evil. The fall of Adam and Eve has caused our will to be weakened and disordered. We become more manipulatable by the devil and his demons.

SCRIPTURE ENCOUNTER – IN ADAM OR IN CHRIST

IN ADAM

Genesis 2: 17 – The toxic effect of the Adam's sin includes death.
> [17] but of the tree of the knowledge of good and evil you shall not eat, for in the day that you eat of it you shall die."

Genesis 3: 7 – Adam and Eves eyes were opened, and they recognized their nakedness.
> [7] Then the eyes of both were opened, and they knew that they were naked.

Genesis 3: 22 – They now knew good and evil.
> [22] Then the LORD God said, "See, the man has become like one of us, knowing good and evil."

Romans 5: 12 – Sin and death came into the world through Adam.
> [12] Therefore, just as sin came into the world through one man, and death came through sin, and so death spread to all because all have sinned—

Psalms 51: 5 – We are born guilty.
> [5] Indeed, I was born guilty, a sinner when my mother conceived me.

IN CHRIST WE ARE A NEW CREATION

Romans 6: 3-5 – By faith in Christ we become a new creation, transformed, and heirs to a new kingdom – a new people.

> ³ Do you not know that all of us who have been baptized into Christ Jesus were baptized into his death? ⁴ Therefore we have been buried with him by baptism into death, so that, just as Christ was raised from the dead by the glory of the Father, so we too might walk in newness of life. ⁵ For if we have been united with him in a death like his, we will certainly be united with him in a resurrection like his.

PREDICTED IN THE OLD TESTAMENT:

Ezekiel 36: 24-27 – Ezekiel prophesies that God will place His Spirit within us.

> ²⁴ I will take you from the nations, and gather you from all the countries, and bring you into your own land. ²⁵ I will sprinkle clean water upon you, and you shall be clean from all your uncleannesses, and from all your idols I will cleanse you. ²⁶ A new heart I will give you, and a new spirit I will put within you; and I will remove from your body the heart of stone and give you a heart of flesh. ²⁷ I will put my spirit within you, and make you follow my statutes and be careful to observe my ordinances.

WHAT IS YOUR UNDERSTANDING FROM THESE SCRIPTURES? HOW DO THESE SCRIPTURES APPLY TO YOU?

_____
_____
_____
_____

In Adam ≈ *Death / Dying*   In Christ ≈ *Life / Living*

We are fallen because of man's hubris. Hubris might be defined as a great or foolish amount of pride or self-confidence.

We do not have perfect order because at first, we are 'in Adam'. In Adam's fall our spiritual nature became separated from God. The consequence of Adam's action was spiritual death, as well as physical death. 'In Christ' we are reunited; we receive healing and life.

4. We Have Free Will and Choice

God gave us free will. With this free will we are left to choose to follow God and His commandments, or follow our own worldly pursuits.

CHOICE LINE

GOD'S LIGHT

CONSCIENCE / CHOICE

DARKNESS
WORLD
FLESH
OURSELVES
EVIL

The choice is left to us, and whatever we choose is what we get. If we choose God, and along with Him Jesus and the Holy Spirit, then we open ourselves to healing and wholeness.

> [14] It was he who created humankind in the beginning, and he left them in the power of their own free choice. [15] If you choose, you can keep the commandments, and to act faithfully is a matter of your own choice. [16] He has placed before you fire and water; stretch out your hand for whichever you choose. [17] Before each person are life and death, and whichever one chooses will be given.
> Sirach 15: 14-17

SCRIPTURE ENCOUNTER – EXAMPLES OF FREE CHOICE IN THE BIBLE

Jeremiah 21: 8

[8] And to this people you shall say: Thus says the LORD: See, I am setting before you the way of life and the way of death.

Deuteronomy 11: 26 -28

[26] See, I am setting before you today a blessing and a curse: [27] the blessing, if you obey the commandments of the LORD your God that I am commanding you today; [28] and the curse, if you do not obey the commandments of the LORD your God, but turn from the way that I am commanding you today, to follow other gods that you have not known.

Deuteronomy 30: 15-20

[15] See, I have set before you today life and prosperity, death and adversity. [16] If you obey the commandments of the LORD your God that I am commanding you today, by loving the LORD your God, walking in his ways, and observing his commandments, decrees, and ordinances, then you shall live and become numerous, and the LORD your God will bless you in the land that you are entering to possess. [17] But if your heart turns away and you do not hear, but are led astray to bow down to other gods and serve them, [18] I declare to you today that you shall perish; you shall not live long in the land that you are crossing the Jordan to enter and possess. [19] I call heaven and earth to witness against you today that I have set before you life and death, blessings and curses. Choose life so that you and your descendants may live, [20] loving the LORD your God, obeying him, and holding fast to him; for that means life to you and length of days, so that you may live in the land that the LORD swore to give to your ancestors, to Abraham, to Isaac, and to Jacob.

HEALING LIFE'S HURTS

FIVE FOLD CYCLE

Method of Healing Personal Hurt

Those who abide in me and I in them bear much fruit

…whichever one chooses will be given.

Sirach 15: 14-17

Just Try It!

FFC works…

WHAT IS YOUR UNDERSTANDING FROM THESE SCRIPTURES? HOW DO THESE SCRIPTURES APPLY TO YOU?

_____

_____

_____

If we choose the world – the flesh, or Mammon – then we will devoid ourselves of wholeness and healing.

The choice is yours; you can't serve two masters (Matthew 6: 24). What will you choose? Stop and think about it.

Whatever you give attention to, whatever you feed, is what grows and develops in your heart and mind. The more we grasp the essence of Christianity, the more we come to realize that everything depends upon the attitude of our will. Do we join the Lord – "Thy Kingdom come"? Do we seek His will – "Thy will be done"?

We are invited by God to join, like a branch to His vine, opening our personal will to the will of God. Our Lord never transgressed a person's will; rather, he showed the path to wholeness and freedom and opened the mind to one's inheritance as children of God.

STUDY NOTES: NOT MY WILL BUT YOURS BE DONE

Review these scriptures. What do they say to you?

Matthew 26: 39 _____

Luke 22: 42 _____

Mark 14: 36 _____

John 6: 38 _____

*I am the vine, you are the branches. Those who abide in me and I in them
bear much fruit, because apart from me you can do nothing.*
John 15: 5

Now, I don't know why the Lord God gave us free choice. If you were God, would you have given humans free choice? But He did, and we have it. And we must put it to good use. How will you use your free will today?

Prayer:
Lord, I give you freedom to work within me…

WORKSHOP # 2

PROCLAMATION:
IN FREE CHOICE WE ACCEPT JESUS AS LORD OF OUR LIFE.

(The answer is yes!)

Do you renounce Satan and all wrong doing? _____

Do you believe that Jesus is the Son of God, that He died to free us from our sins and that He rose to bring us new life? _____

Will you follow Jesus as your Lord? _____

Do you proclaim, Lord Jesus, as your personal Lord and Savior? _____

Please read Appendix 'F' – PRAYER FOR SALVATION
(This will help confirm your decision to accept Jesus as Lord of your life.)

Take a moment to review!

What have you learned to this point in the exercises and readings?

_____

_____

_____

_____

_____

_____

_____

_____

_____

_____

_____

_____

Paula Sandford in her book *Healing Victims of Sexual Abuse* had a statement that seems to be important when we think of 'choice'. She said "Healing, restoration and holiness are not accomplished by striving". And further she wrote: "From the beginning, we came to realize that true restoration of relationships involved more than mental choices to forgive and be forgiven, and a great deal more than fleshly striving to be kind and loving. Holiness is not achieved merely by working to order our behavior according to the laws of God. Holiness is a matter of giving ourselves so completely to the Lordship of Jesus Christ that by the power of His Spirit living in us we are transformed into His likeness." (Please refer to Supplemental Readings - Appendix 'D' for information on her book.)

5. The Separation of Body, Mind, Soul, and Spirit

We have four basic components:

      i) Body
      ii) Mind
      iii) Soul [3]
      iv) Spirit

If we think of ourselves as these components, then we can more easily understand how choice affects us. As well, we can see how wholeness is accomplished and healing occurs. Watch how your choices affect the different components.

When we make a decision for Christ and the Trinity, our spirit is immediately healed and is united with the Lord. It is the first conversion experience.

$$\text{OUR SPIRIT} \approx \text{THE HOLY SPIRIT}$$

This is the conversion experience, or 'born again' experience that Christians talk about. Something happens and we feel good. Of course, we feel good – how else could we feel in the presence of the Lord?

You see, with the fall of Adam and Eve, we were separated from the Lord (Genesis 3: 23+). With our free will we can allow our spirit to be reunited with the Lord.

> *Q 1*
> *Born Again.*

THE BODY

When we make a decision for Christ, our spirit is joined with the Lord, but what has happened to our body? Nothing! Our body is still the same size and same height as it was before. If we had ulcers, we still have ulcers. If we were fat, we still are fat. The conversion did not change our body.

We are told to make it a temple fitting the indwelling of the Holy Spirit (1 Corinthians 6: 19 -20).

SCRIPTURE ENCOUNTER – OUR TEMPLE

1 Corinthians 3: 16-17 – You are God's Temple and God's Spirit dwells in you
[16] Do you not know that you are God's temple and that God's Spirit dwells in you? [17] If anyone destroys God's temple, God will destroy that person. For God's temple is holy, and you are that temple.

1 Corinthians 6: 19-20 – The Body is a Temple of the Holy Spirit
[19] Or do you not know that your body is a temple of the Holy Spirit within you, which you have from God, and that you are not your own? [20] For you were bought with a price; therefore glorify God in your body.

WHAT IS YOUR UNDERSTANDING FROM THESE SCRIPTURES?

_____
_____
_____
_____

This means we are to start taking care of our body - eating right, sleeping right, exercising and caring for it. As we do this, our body comes into oneness with our soul.

You might read the meditation in Appendix 'G' entitled *God's Temple Is In You*.

Q 2
Need to Heal the Body.

WORKSHOP # 3
– <u>TARGETING OUR BODY POINTS</u>

TARGETS IN OUR BODY

What areas in your body need the Lord's healing to make it a worthy temple for the indwelling of the Holy Spirit?

(An example here is that I have a little pot-belly and am about 20 pounds' overweight. My target then is to get rid of the weight. The habit that needs my attention has two parts: one is eating moderately and the second daily exercise.)

(Another example might be that my shoulder is always aching because I worry. I am going to go into prayer and source the worry, when I feel the discomfort in my shoulder.)

<u>Targets that need my attention:</u>   <u>Habits I need to nourish:</u>

1. _____   _____

2. _____   _____

3. _____   _____

THE MIND

What about our mind? There is no change that we notice, or is there? We still have the same thoughts we had before, and the same feelings emoted by those thoughts. If we were hurt by someone – for example, if we were sexually abused – we still remember it. We still feel angry, fearful, guilty, mistrusting, hateful towards men or women, have sexual problems, etc. So is our mind the same? We still think about things that are not of God; we still feel anxious, worried, and impatient. So clearly the Fruit of the Spirit [4] is not present, and therefore our mind hasn't changed. Or has it?

Yes, there *has* been a change. There are new thoughts. When we made the decision for the Lord, the Holy Spirit gave us gifts. Only at this point, they are not encompassing our life. Many of the gifts have not been activated.

Our potential is not yet actualized.

THE SOUL

What about the Soul?[5] Has it changed? No. We still are burdened by the residue of sin that has not been confessed. Things that we have done wrong outside of God's love still plague us, and affect both our mind (guilt) and our body.

Sin is a barrier in our relationship to God, it inhibits us from receiving His blessings and gifts. Sin only disappears when we bring them to Jesus on the Cross. We apply Jesus' blood and apprehend the blessings. When this is done the legal issue that has limited us is removed – the Devil has no more legal right. The barrier removed allows blessings and healing to flow.

WORKSHOP # 4
– Forgiveness: *(Forgiveness means surrender.)*

I. Write down 5 of the worst experiences of your life.
(These worst experiences could be sins. Bring each to Jesus. Work on one at a time.)

_____

_____

_____

_____

_____

II. What are the most uncomfortable experiences of your life? (If you are uncomfortable with an event, you may need more (self) forgiveness.)

_____

_____

_____

(Take these issues both 5 worst experiences and most uncomfortable experiences of your life through the prayer on the next page. Repent and release them to God, your Father, and ask for forgiveness and healing.)

Prayer:

FOR A FORGIVING HEART

Father, I ask You to take judgment and bitterness out of my life.

I forgive *(Fill In The Blank)* _____ for hurting me.

I do not want this in my life – I repent and ask You to remove it. Heal my heart – forgive my sin.

I receive your forgiveness.

Father, forgive my anger, resentment, bitterness and unforgiveness.

From this day forward, I resolve not to judge others and I put their actions on the Cross. I place *(Fill In The Blank)* _____ into your hands.

I proclaim my trust in You alone, my God. You are the Righteous Judge.

Father, bless _____ in every way.

In Jesus, I thank you Father. Amen.

THE SPIRIT

Next, we will look at the Spirit. In the previous chapters the following statements were made:

- We focus on an issue or problem, asking for the Lord's help through His Holy Spirit. The Holy Spirit guides us as we take it to the Lord in prayer, asking for cleansing/pruning. Page 3
- We are all Broken People. Page 5
- There was an exchange on the Cross of Jesus. Page 8
- If we choose God, and along with Him, Jesus and the Holy Spirit, then we open ourselves to healing and wholeness. Page 14
- The more we grasp the essence of Christianity, the more we come to realize that everything depends upon the attitude of our will. Page 16
- We are told to make it (our body) a temple fitting the indwelling of the Holy Spirit. Page 20
- In our mind there are new thoughts. We see a new potential. The Holy Spirit has given us gifts. Page 21
- We see sin as a barrier in our relationship to God. Forgiveness is needed. Page 22

There is an underlying understanding and expectation that you have opened to the Holy Spirit in your life, that you have a relationship with the Holy Spirit and that you can hear and follow Spirit's direction to guide, form and heal your life.

We are not driven by circumstances of our life but always look forward to God's design in each situation. We cannot control the events of our life but we can control our reactions and apply God's prescriptions.

God has given us the capacity to collaborate with His Holy Spirit – the ability to work with His Spirit. When we collaborate, we choose to lay our self-will down and listen. Collaboration here means being one with the Spirit.

STUDY NOTES: COLLABORATE WITH HOLY SPIRIT

Review these scriptures. What do they say to you?

Luke 9: 23 _____

Galatians 5: 24-25 _____

2 Corinthians 5: 17 _____

Ephesians 4: 22-24 _____

Now the Lord is the Spirit, and where the Spirit of the Lord is, there is freedom.
2 Corinthians 3: 17

We will now look at scripture to understand the availability and purpose of interaction of the Holy Spirit in our life. Then you will be invited to pray for the Baptism in the Spirit – yielding to the presence and power of the Holy Spirit.

> *Q 3*
> *The Spirit.*

SCRIPTURE ENCOUNTER
– AVAILABILITY OF THE HOLY SPIRIT:

This section is meant to give you an understanding of the importance of receiving the Holy Spirit. The Holy Spirit is the Gift from God the Father. Scripture predicted that Jesus would Baptize by the Spirit and that the Spirit would be with us forever.

Matthew 3: 11 – John the Baptist prophecies that Jesus will Baptize in the Spirit
[11] "I baptize you with water for repentance, but one who is more powerful than I is coming after me; I am not worthy to carry his sandals. He will baptize you with the Holy Spirit and fire.

Mark 1: 7-8 – John the Baptist proclaims that Jesus will baptize in the Holy Spirit.
[7] He proclaimed, "The one who is more powerful than I is coming after me; I am not worthy to stoop down and untie the thong of his sandals. [8] I have baptized you with water; but he will baptize you with the Holy Spirit."

Luke 3: 16 – John baptizes with water but Jesus with the Holy Spirit and fire.
[16] John answered all of them by saying, "I baptize you with water; but one who is more powerful than I is coming; I am not worthy to untie the thong of his sandals. He will baptize you with the Holy Spirit and fire.

John 1: 29-34 – John testifies to Jesus as the Son of God, the one who Baptizes with the Holy Spirit.
[29] The next day he saw Jesus coming toward him and declared, "Here is the Lamb of God who takes away the sin of the world! [30] This is he of whom I said, 'After me comes a man who ranks ahead of me because he was before me.' [31] I myself did not know him; but I came baptizing with water for this reason, that he might be revealed to Israel." [32] And John testified, "I saw the Spirit descending from heaven like a dove, and it remained on him. [33] I myself did not know him, but the one who sent me to baptize with water said to me, 'He on whom you see the Spirit descend and remain is the one who baptizes with the Holy Spirit.' [34] And I myself have seen and have testified that this is the Son of God."

John 14: 16 – Jesus says He will ask the Father and the Father will send the Holy Spirit.
[16] And I will ask the Father, and he will give you another Advocate, to be with you forever.

Ephesians 3: 14-17 – Paul's prayer for his readers to receive the Spirit

¹⁴ For this reason I bow my knees before the Father, ¹⁵ from whom every family in heaven and on earth takes its name. ¹⁶ I pray that, according to the riches of his glory, he may grant that you may be strengthened in your inner being with power through his Spirit, ¹⁷ and that Christ may dwell in your hearts through faith, as you are being rooted and grounded in love.

WHAT IS YOUR UNDERSTANDING FROM THESE SCRIPTURES?

_____

_____

_____

_____

Father John H. Hampsch, C.M.F.,[6] explains the position in which we find ourselves as 'not fully operative'. The gifts and fruit of the Holy Spirit are available to us, but we have not put them into use. Fr. Hampsch explained it as like receiving a gift from a friend and placing it upon a shelf. We have the gift, but it is still fully packaged and wrapped.

If you do not understand what is meant by gifts and fruit of the Holy Spirit, I recommend you review Appendix 'B'. If you are Catholic you might read Fr. Robert DeGrandis' books: *Introduction to the Catholic Charismatic Renewal, Growth in the Spirit,* and *Layperson's Manual for the Healing Ministry*.[7] If you are Protestant or Anglican/Episcopal, I recommend you read Dennis and Rita Bennett's books: *Nine o'clock In The Morning, The Holy Spirit and You,* and *Trinity of Man*.[8] As General Editor, I re-published a book entitled *You Can Minister Spiritual Gifts* by Thomas W. Roycroft[9] which is a good resource to understand the Gifts of the Holy Spirit.

Our job then is to learn to use the gifts of the Holy Spirit and to begin to live in the fruit of the Holy Spirit. Appendix 'B' is meant as an introduction to the Holy Spirit and describes the Gifts.

What can I do to receive the Holy Spirit? What can I do to receive the Baptism in the Holy Spirit? On the next page you will find a prayer that will help you to yield to the Holy Spirit and His gifts.

In humility we approach Jesus and ask for the Baptism in the Holy Spirit.

We are encouraged to ask for this gift **often** – Born again and again. The Book of Acts records at least seven times that the apostles were filled with the Holy Spirit (Acts 2: 4; 4: 8; 4: 31; 6: 8; 7: 55; 13: 9 and 13: 52). You might refer to the Scripture Encounter entitled Availability of the Holy Spirit on page 25 and Appendix 'G'– Receiving The Holy Spirit – Baptism In The Holy Spirit.

Q 4
Baptism in the Spirit

Prayer:
FOR THE BAPTISM IN THE SPIRIT

If you have never been Baptized in the Holy Spirit you might pray these prayers.

YIELDING TO THE BAPTISM-IN-THE-SPIRIT

Lord Jesus, I repent of my sins and proclaimed you as my personal Lord and Savior. I humbly ask you to baptize me in your Holy Spirit. I Ask you to fill me with the living waters of your Spirit. I claim the Promise you made that if we ask, we will receive. I am now asking Lord, in faith, come Holy Spirit and baptize me in your Spirit.

PRAYER FOR GIFTS

Holy Spirit, please release in me now all other gifts that you see fit. So that I may be equipped to lead a full Christian life and be of service to the community. I ask you Lord to enrich me with the Gifts of Tongues, Word of Wisdom, Word of Knowledge, Faith, Healing, Miracles, Prophecy, Discernment of Spirits, Public Tongues and Interpretation.

THANKSGIVING PRAYER

Thank you Jesus for baptizing me in your Holy Spirit. To you be the glory. Amen.

One must realize at this point that all four areas, body, mind, soul and spirit, are inter-related and therefore affect each other. As you look at the Web Theory below it will explain this idea.

The Web Theory

It is like a spider web. Every strand is inter-connected to every other strand. Our life is like a web of experiences, memories, emotions, and reactions.

It is easy to see it when we think of how our mind and body are connected, for instance, when we worry, we can end up with ulcers. It is a little more difficult to see the other side. An example might be that when we have an injury or the flu, it affects our ability to concentrate and think straight.

In similar ways the soul affects the body and mind and is affected by the body and the mind in return.

I would guess by this point you are getting the drift - choices affect us in our relationship with the Lord. If we are not in the light of the Lord, then we open ourselves to problems. We have made the wrong choices.

But the path of the righteous is like the light of dawn, which shines brighter and brighter until full day. The way of the wicked is like deep darkness; they do not know what they stumble over.
Proverbs 4:18-19

When we choose the Lord, our spirit is immediately united with Him. This starts the process of the conversion of the other areas of mind, body, and soul.

WORKSHOP # 5

– <u>ENVISION YOURSELF IN HEAVEN</u>.

Envision yourself in Heaven. See yourself in eternity.
Notice your eyes and your hair and your clothing.
You have that glow as you reflect Jesus, the son of God.
What is your demeanor?
Are you experiencing His Joy – His Spirit's Fruit?

>   Every burden has been lifted.
>   Every sickness removed.
>   Every inner hurt healed.
>   Sin is gone from your life – the battle has ended.

Through the obstacles of your present life, Jesus is trying to show us this vision of ourselves as we will be.

God will not stop until His transforming work is finished.

DESCRIBE YOUR EXPERIENCE:

_____
_____
_____

Christ in you the hope of glory! Colossians 1:27

Scripture tells us to renew our minds; we are told to put on new minds and get rid of the old. This means that we are to allow the Lord's light into old memories, old emotions, old thoughts, and the old automatic behaviors we are used to. As we do this, the Lord starts to renew those thoughts, memories, and emotions. The old automatic behaviors (reactions, retorts, and reflexes) are transformed and changed in the Lord's light. So gradually, our mind is renewed and brought into unity.

SCRIPTURE ENCOUNTER

– NEW AND RADICAL CHANGE

2 Corinthians 5: 17 – Brand new person.
^{17} So if anyone is in Christ, there is a new creation: everything old has passed away; see, everything has become new!

Ephesians 4: 22-24 – Put away the old self and be renewed in the spirit of your minds.
^{22} You were taught to put away your former way of life, your old self, corrupt and deluded by its lusts, ^{23} and to be renewed in the spirit of your minds, ^{24} and to clothe yourselves with the new self, created according to the likeness of God in true righteousness and holiness.

Ephesians 5: 8 – Be children of the light.
^{8} For once you were darkness, but now in the Lord you are light. Live as children of light—

Romans 8: 5 – Direction to set your minds on the Spirit.
^{5} For those who live according to the flesh set their minds on the things of the flesh, but those who live according to the Spirit set their minds on the things of the Spirit.

1 Thessalonians 5: 23-24 – He will sanctify you and He is faithful.
^{23} May the God of peace himself sanctify you entirely; and may your spirit and soul and body be kept sound and blameless at the coming of our Lord Jesus Christ. ^{24} The one who calls you is faithful, and he will do this.

WHAT IS YOUR UNDERSTANDING FROM THESE SCRIPTURES?

___

___

___

___

Pain and trauma in our life is often a pathway to sin, but we have the option to transform it and use it as an opportunity to encounter God.

Q 5

I am afraid of change.

WORKSHOP # 6

– <u>GET RID OF OLD HABITS</u>

Have you ever just lost it? You look back and say, 'what was that'? Others might say 'what happened to you'? We all do this. It is those old feelings, those old events, that still lay below the surface.

There is this cute little phrase that goes like this: 'You can often tell what makes a person tick by the way they unwind.'

LIST THE OLD HABITS THAT NEGATIVELY IMPACT YOUR LIFE:

_____

_____

_____

_____

BRING EACH ONE THROUGH THE FIVE FOLD CYCLE

– ASKING THE LORD'S HEALING

(You may refer to Appendix 'A'- Five Fold Cycle – Method of Healing Personal Hurt)

In the same manner as scripture tells us to renew our minds, we are also told to make our body a temple of the Holy Spirit. This means we are to re-evaluate how we are taking care of our bodies; we must start making them temples worthy of the Holy Spirit. This means eating right, sleeping right, exercising, and caring for our bodies; it may also mean medical care. We start to renew our bodies and bring them into unity.

SCRIPTURE ENCOUNTER

– BODY IS THE TEMPLE OF THE HOLY SPIRIT:

John 14: 15-17 – The Advocate abides in you.
[15] "If you love me, you will keep my commandments. [16] And I will ask the Father, and he will give you another Advocate, to be with you forever. [17] This is the Spirit of truth, whom the world cannot receive, because it neither sees him nor knows him. You know him, because he abides with you, and he will be in you.

Romans 12: 1-2 – Present your bodies as a living sacrifice, holy and acceptable to God.
[1] I appeal to you therefore, brothers and sisters, by the mercies of God, to present your bodies as a living sacrifice, holy and acceptable to God, which is your spiritual worship. [2] Do not be conformed to this world, but be transformed by the renewing of your minds, so that you may discern what is the will of God—what is good and acceptable and perfect.

1 Corinthians 6: 19-20 – Glorify God in your body.
[19] Or do you not know that your body is a temple of the Holy Spirit within you, which you have from God, and that you are not your own? [20] For you were bought with a price; therefore glorify God in your body.

WHAT IS YOUR UNDERSTANDING FROM THESE SCRIPTURES?

_____
_____
_____
_____

Like the mind and body, the soul, as the collector of sin, needs to be cleansed. We need to bring each and every sin to the Lord's light and ask forgiveness. As we cleanse the sin, the soul becomes united with the other parts.

Gradually, all the parts of body, mind, soul, and spirit, come in to unity and oneness with the Lord through the Holy Spirit.

There is a relation between the well-being of the Spirit
and the well-being of the body. 3 John 1: 2

Until we bring the parts into unity with the Spirit there is dissonance, and the dissonance causes confusion and unsettled feelings. Often this dissonance leads people to think that they were not saved by their decision for the Lord. The problem is that they did not follow through on their choice; they did not cleanse the body, mind, and soul.

We must take each area to the Lord, little by little, and bring it under His Light and Lordship (His rule). Each is a mini-conversion experience – dying to self, renewing the old.

DIAGRAM - FOUR BASIC COMPONENTS EXPLAINED

BODY ≈ Temple of the Holy Spirit

MIND ≈ Old Thoughts, Patterns/Behaviors, Memories and the Emotions tied to them.
New Thoughts and Impulses

SOUL ≈ Sins and Blessings

---------------------- Line of Dissonance ----------------------

SPIRIT ≈ God's Spirit

STUDY NOTES: WE ARE SPIRIT FIRST

What do these lines mean to you?

Jeremiah 1: 5 _____

Psalm 139: 13 _____
& Jeremiah 1: 5

1 Corinthians 3: 16 _____
& 2 Corinthians 1: 22

Genesis 1: 27 _____

For in him we live, and move, and have our being. . . Acts 17:28

6. Choices

The very first choice which predisposes all others is a choice for Christ Jesus. Underlying that is our understanding that Jesus is God and the second Person of the Blessed Trinity (God the Father, Son, and Holy Spirit).

The next stage of choice is turning to God in each event of our life: thought, word, and action. All are mini-conversion experiences. In this way we can begin to experience the new man, and the radical change that Christ promised.

A profound interior conversion.

A friend and I were climbing a mountain one day, and as we approached the summit of a ridge he became gripped by fear, which had been building up as we climbed higher and higher. The fear was now overpowering and he was anxious and sweating, holding onto the bushes and trees for all his worth. I had known about his fear of heights, but he had never let me pray. I always assumed he would do the healing prayer himself. The fear, however, had taken him over and he was not enjoying the mountain nor the view from the ridge that looked down to a pristine lake. I offered to pray.

Now you will note that I use the word "simple" when referring to the things of God – because the things of God *are* simple. Read, for example, this scripture: 'perfect love casts out fear' – or we might say 'Love drives out all fear' (1 John 4: 18). It is a simple equation – love and fear are opposites. But back to the story.

We stopped, closed our eyes, focused on the fear, and looked for the source. The source turned out to be an incident that occurred when he was a young farm boy; he was jumping off the front of a swather and fell, hitting the dirt. It was a small incident in a child's life, but left him with a fear of heights. This fear developed and increased as he grew up.

He had a choice: to keep the fear, or to let the Lord into it. We prayed, asking the Lord into the memory – bringing it to the light. We asked for His grace and peace to fill the boy and commanded the fear to leave. It took only a moment; the fear left and the mountain experiences from then on became exhilarating. It is funny how simple that was in the Lord Jesus!

The key is that when you run into an obstacle, you open to God's healing through Jesus' redemptive act on the Cross and that you allow the Holy Spirit to be your guide.

WORKSHOP # 7

- **<u>IDENTITY IN CHRIST JESUS</u>**

WHO ARE YOU IN JESUS CHRIST? *You might refer to Appendix 'H'*
_____

WHAT DOES HE CALL YOU? (BY WHAT NAME DOES HE CALL YOU?)
_____

WHAT IS YOUR IMAGE OF JESUS?
_____

WHAT IS JESUS IMAGE OF YOU?
_____

DO YOU HAVE A RELATIONSHIP WITH JESUS?
_____

These are all questions that speak to us about our identity in Jesus. These questions speak about a relationship with Jesus. In Jesus we have a special place. We have been called and predestined to be adopted children. As adopted children we have the rights of children within that family. As you read the Scripture Encounter below and pay attention to this question: "What does it say about your position in Christ?"

> *Q 6*
> *It's all about relationship.*

SCRIPTURE ENCOUNTER

– ADOPTION

Ephesians 1: 3-14 – Adoption (NIV)

³ Praise be to the God and Father of our Lord Jesus Christ, who has blessed us in the heavenly realms with every spiritual blessing in Christ.

⁴ For he chose us in him before the creation of the world to be holy and blameless in his sight. In love

⁵ he predestined us to be adopted as his sons through Jesus Christ, in accordance with his pleasure and will--

⁶ to the praise of his glorious grace, which he has freely given us in the One he loves.

⁷ In him we have redemption through his blood, the forgiveness of sins, in accordance with the riches of God's grace

⁸ that he lavished on us with all wisdom and understanding.

⁹ And he {With all wisdom and understanding,} made known to us the mystery of his will according to his good pleasure, which he purposed in Christ,

¹⁰ to be put into effect when the times will have reached their fulfillment-- to bring all things in heaven and on earth together under one head, even Christ.

¹¹ In him we were also chosen, {were made heirs} having been predestined according to the plan of him who works out everything in conformity with the purpose of his will,

¹² in order that we, who were the first to hope in Christ, might be for the praise of his glory.

¹³ And you also were included in Christ when you heard the word of truth, the gospel of your salvation. Having believed, you were marked in him with a seal, the promised Holy Spirit,

¹⁴ who is a deposit guaranteeing our inheritance until the redemption of those who are God's possession-- to the praise of his glory.

WHAT DOES EPHESIANS 1 SAY ABOUT YOUR POSITION IN CHRIST?"

(Especially pay attention to the underlined portions.)

_____
_____
_____
_____
_____
_____
_____
_____

Take a break now and go to Appendix 'H' & 'I'. Task yourself to complete the two workshops to identify your Identity and Position in Christ.

What are the scripture(s) that define your Identity in Christ? (Who am I in Christ?)

_____
_____
_____
_____

What are the scripture(s) that define your Position in Christ? (I am with Christ therefore ...)

_____
_____
_____
_____

Prayer:

FOR ADOPTION

Lord, as Your adopted child, I ask You to come into my heart and let me experience the closeness of this relationship with You …

Lord, You created my inmost being; You knit me together in my mother's womb. I praise You because I am fearfully and wonderfully made: Your works are wonderful, (Psalm 139: 13-14)

I will be strong and courageous. I will not be afraid, for You Lord go with me; You will never leave me nor forsake me… (Deuteronomy 31:6)

Lord, help me to become all You created me to be …

Thank you for adopting me…

7. So Let's Review

We are all broken people because we are the products of broken people – our parents. We all receive the effects of being 'in Adam'. We are told in scripture to come to be 'in Jesus'. We are told to join Him as a branch is joined to a tree, and that the Father will cleanse and prune us. That old song 'What A Friend We Have In Jesus' spoke about Jesus as our friend, bearing our sins and griefs. All we have to do is carry them to Him in prayer. When we don't, we suffer needless pain. It is simple.

In Romans we remember:

That "In Adam all have sinned/ died."
Romans 5: 12-14

And that "In Christ all receive life"
Romans 5: 15-19

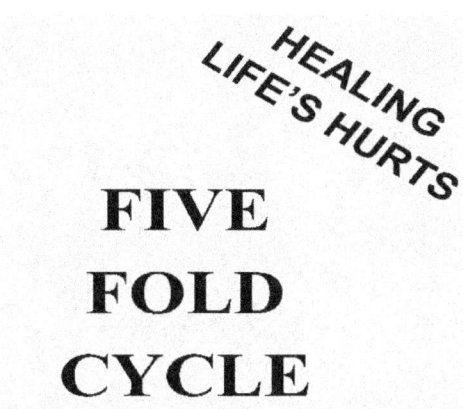

We learned that we have free will and that we have choices before us. The choices affect us by bringing us under the Lord's light and healing influence, or by inhibiting our ability to receive His love. The results of our choices, and the resultant thoughts, words, and actions, affect our body, mind, soul, and spirit. They are all interactive like the lines of a spider web. Therefore, choices affect our relationship with the Lord.

In each incident in our life, we must choose to move closer to Christ and away from darkness. We do this by involving Him in each incident, each memory, each feeling, and each thought. As He comes into each of these incidents or events, whether in the present or the past, we are transformed by His light.

Always look at the light not the shadow.

The shadow is looking back at our failure, our dark side. We always want to be looking to Heaven – looking to the light. It is when we look up to Jesus that we find a way out of self.

> We are all broken people because we are products of broken people...
>
> In Christ all receive life...
>
> We are transformed by His light.

Just Try It!

FFC works...

Be Holy.

A PIE

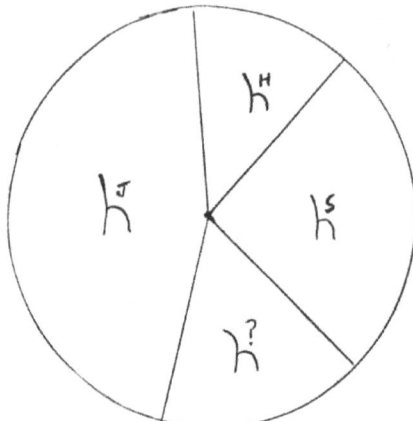

The image of a homemade pie helps me to understand this concept. Picture a pie with pieces cut by some well-intentioned young child. Notice they are irregular and that there are some good size pieces for us sweet-tooths.

Now let us say this pie represents your relationship with the Lord. In each section something has to be on the throne. Is it you, God, Money, the World, or what?

Jesus, the Messiah, came to free those bound-up and offers a relationship with God – like His own. Jesus offers to reconnect us to His Father. Our separation and the renewal offered in Jesus Christ is described in these Scriptures – where we are told to move *from Death to Life*:

> [1] You were dead through the trespasses and sins [2] in which you once lived, following the course of this world, following the ruler of the power of the air, the spirit that is now at work among those who are disobedient. [3] All of us once lived among them in the passions of our flesh, following the desires of flesh and senses, and we were by nature children of wrath, like everyone else. [4] But God, who is rich in mercy, out of the great love with which he loved us [5] even when we were dead through our trespasses, made us alive together with Christ—by grace you have been saved—
> Ephesians 2: 1-5

And also, we are told to move from the *Old Life to the New Life:*

> [17] Now this I affirm and insist on in the Lord: you must no longer live as the Gentiles live, in the futility of their minds. [18] They are darkened in their understanding, alienated from the life of God because of their ignorance and hardness of heart. . . [20] That is not the way you learned Christ!
> Ephesians 4: 17-20

Put Jesus – 'J' – on the throne in the largest piece of pie. That is where most Christians would have Him. So, in reality, Jesus owns the majority of the pie. But who is on the throne in the other pieces? I put an 'H' on the throne in one piece. That might represent a hurt that you have had in life. Because we were hurt, we did not receive what we needed in that portion of our life. I explain it this way: Jesus wasn't fully able to touch this incident or event, or He wasn't *fully* in that incident or event. If we didn't experience love, joy, peace, and patience - the fruit of the spirit, then Jesus' healing touch was inhibited. That is why we feel hurt.

Look at another section of the pie. I put an 'S' on that one. It stands for 'sex.' In my life, and I am sure in the lives of others, Jesus didn't always have control of our sex life. Therefore, he wasn't on the throne. We have to let him on the throne in the present and in the past. As He heals us, He will take over that portion of the pie, and we gradually nibble away at the problem areas.

We want the Lord to take over all our lives and be active in each portion of the pie. Then we will be in unity, and we will find love, joy, peace - The fruit of the Spirit – flowing throughout us, body, mind, soul and spirit. The Lord will make our personalities more integrated and more whole. Follow the Spirit who will nurture in us what is good and keep safe what He has nurtured.

There is a spiritual law that applies to our lives:

Spiritual Law – Negatives are not Under Jesus' Rule

If you find that any Portion of your Life does not have the Fruit of the Spirit, then Jesus isn't fully present. We are chosen and appointed to live and act within the Spirit's influence.

[16] You did not choose me but I chose you. And I appointed you to go and bear fruit, fruit that will last, so that the Father will give you whatever you ask him in my name.
John 15: 16

WORKSHOP # 8

– FRUIT OF THE SPIRIT

What are the Fruit of the Spirit?   Galatians 5: 22-23

L____ , J____ , P____ , _____

List the areas in your life where the Fruit of the Spirit are not evident:

_____

_____

_____

You are now starting to identify areas where you must apply the Five Fold Cycle.

Paul put it quite succinctly in Ephesians, where he told us to take off the old and put on the new:

> [22] You were taught to put away your former way of life, your old self, corrupt and deluded by its lusts, [23] and to be renewed in the spirit of your minds, [24] and to clothe yourselves with the new self, created according to the likeness of God in true righteousness and holiness." Ephesians 4: 22-24

Paul tells us to put on a new mind, and he tells us to transform our mind. He is talking about a process of overcoming the old self – the Old Man. As we go through this process, we become renewed, but it is not instantaneous. In the born-again experience we feel a change and often it stays with us for quite a while. But gradually the old feeling, thoughts, and actions come back to haunt us. There is a dissonance between the areas where Christ is on the throne and the other parts of our lives. That is where inner healing comes in to fill the gap. Jesus' love is not caught up in time and space; He can 'renew' our minds, our hurts, and our bodies. All we have to do is allow Him into the negative things in our lives.

Dissonance – Pay attention to where there is tension in your life. Dissonance $\approx$ Tension.

There is a second spiritual law that reassures us that even the most hideous sin can be renewed by the Lord's love:

Spiritual Law – God Uses all Things

God Uses all Things Unto Good for Those who Love Him.

The story of Joseph, who was sold into slavery, is a fine example of how God can use anything unto good. He repeats this promise at least three times in scripture (Romans 8: 28, Isaiah 38: 17, Genesis 50: 20).

We must take heart and trust in the unfailing love of the Lord who will transform us.

In Part II the workbook will outline the process involved in the *Method of Healing Personal Hurt:* called *Five Fold Cycle*.

CHRIST BEFORE THY DOOR IS WAITING

Christ Before Thy Door Is Waiting by W. Rainer, circa 1883.

II. PROCESS

We will now look at a step-by-step *Method of Healing Personal Hurt*, called: *Five Fold Cycle*.

Step One: Becoming God Focused

The Lord lives in the praises of his people.
(Author Unknown)

I am not sure where that phrase came from, but it is obvious that as we turn our attention to the Lord, He joins with us in a special way.

> Listen! I am standing at the door, knocking; if you hear my voice and open the door, I will come in to you and eat with you, and you with me.
> Revelation 3: 20

Turning to God is using our free will, to open ourselves to the Lord. It reminds me of the painting of Christ standing outside the door and knocking. If we do not open the door, he will not come in.

Often in these paintings there is no doorknob on the side where Jesus Christ is standing. The artist is implying that we must open the door – that our choice opens the door, and that Christ waits patiently, arms outstretched and with His love flowing. All we need to do is open the door a little way or throw it wide open. It is up to us to choose.

> So I say to you, Ask, and it will be given you; search, and you will find; knock, and the door will be opened for you.
> Luke 11: 9

I refer to this repeatedly, because asking is the 'key' to personal healing in Christ. Each time we ask we are choosing God, and therefore we are receiving more, finding more, and opening more. Each is a mini-conversion experience. The first step we must take is to focus on God. We pray and praise Him in whatever way is natural to us, and the Lord will hear.

> [14] And this is the boldness we have in him, that if we ask anything according to his will, he hears us. [15] And if we know that he hears us in whatever we ask, we know that we have obtained the requests made of him.
> 1 John 5: 14-15

> *Q 8*
> *Why use the process?*

SCRIPTURE ENCOUNTER

– ASKING AND RECEIVING

Scriptures on Asking and Receiving:

John 14: 13-14 – Jesus will do whatever we ask so that the Father is glorified.
[13] I will do whatever you ask in my name, so that the Father may be glorified in the Son. [14] If in my name you ask me for anything, I will do it.

Matthew 7: 7-8 – Ask and it will be given, seek and you will find, knock and it will be opened.
[7] Ask, and it will be given you; search, and you will find; knock, and the door will be opened for you. [8] For everyone who asks receives, and everyone who searches finds, and for everyone who knocks, the door will be opened.

1 John 3: 21-22 – We are to bring our hearts into Truth so that they do not condemn us and then we will receive what we ask.
[21] Beloved, if our hearts do not condemn us, we have boldness before God; [22] and we receive from him whatever we ask, because we obey his commandments and do what pleases him.

WHAT IS YOUR UNDERSTANDING FROM THESE SCRIPTURES?

_____
_____
_____
_____

I remember an incident at a weekend youth event. It was late in the evening, and I came to the top landing of a set of stairs to find a teen sitting with his legs dangling through the banister. His head was down, and he seemed troubled, separated from the group. I approached him to find out how he was doing, and he said he had a headache. Now I know headaches are no problem for the Lord, so I asked him if I could pray for him. The young man had not prayed but was very open to it. We prayed for just a moment but that was all it took – the headache was gone. I remember his excitement and his witness, as he ran around the place telling everyone what had just happened. All that was needed was one thing – simply turning to God and asking for His help!

WORKSHOP # 9
– Becoming God Focused

Becoming God Focused – inviting Him into the problem.

Jesus stands at the door and knocks. He waits for us to open the door. The handle is on our side. We are challenged to take some action. It takes courage!

I remember Robin, a young lady, who always felt there was a plexiglass wall between herself, God and the world at large. When she asked God in, He didn't just walk up in front of her or take the plexiglass away. He came gently and slide up beside her. Very comfortable and non-intrusive. It was such a wonderful vision of God's love and nurturing.

I remember a young man's vision. He was at the edge of a cliff above a deep gorge and God told him to step forward. Each time he stepped forward, a piece of land would appear under his feet. As He opened to God and released his fears, he could walk across to the other side.

What are the chains that prohibit you from inviting Christ into the situation?

In your imagination, see yourself at the door.

1. What are the chains that inhibit or prohibit you from opening the door? List them below.
2. What action is then predicated – what actions are required?
   (Ask the Holy Spirit for these inspirations.)

CHAINS: **ACTION YOU MUST TAKE:**

_____   _____

_____   _____

_____   _____

3. Bring each chain to the Lord Jesus on His Cross and place them in His hands.

_____

_____

4. Ask Jesus for the grace to heal the situation. The power to complete the action. What happens as you envision Him touching the situation?

_____

_____

5. Resolve to complete the action and set a timetable and goal.

Set a Timetable and your Goal:

_____

_____

Step Two: Identify a Problem or Issue

(a) Identify

At this point we identify a problem we are having in our life, or an issue which is interfering with our peaceful walk with the Lord.

It has become evident to me and my colleagues that you have to pick small things and be as specific as possible.

Now I know the Lord can do anything He wants. If He can create you, me, and the world, He could fix something as complex as a marital problem; but it doesn't seem to work that way. It seems that our job is to divide the big events into smaller events. It is like dissecting a specimen in biology.

WEDGE

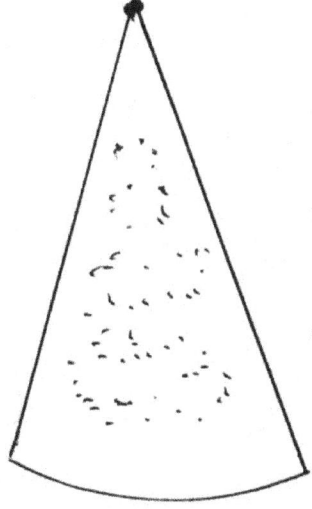

A picture here would be useful. First, think of a marriage as a dot, where two people come together. Then as their marriage progresses, little problems and issues come up. I call that "garbage". The garbage builds up, separating the two lines (people). It ends up looking like a wedge from the pie, with all sorts of junk in the middle.

Now the garbage can be as little as not resolving the issue around how to clean your tooth brush, or how to squeeze the toothpaste tube. The issue just gets packed away and is not resolved. It is just another speck of garbage.

But sooner or later the garbage can gets full, and then it becomes overwhelming.

In the problem-solving process, it is necessary to be specific and begin to nibble away at the issues one at a time. As you do this, the lines (people) come together, as represented in the diagram below, entitled "Nibble Theory".

NIBBLE THEORY

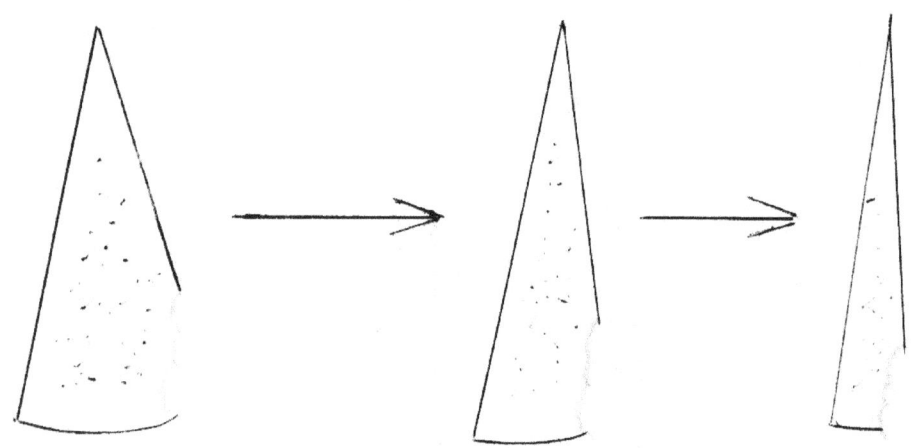

Q 9
Be specific!

(b) Sources

In the process of identification, we want to get to the root of the problem – we are looking for the source. If you can get to the root of the problem, you and the Lord can clean it up.

PLASTER THEORY

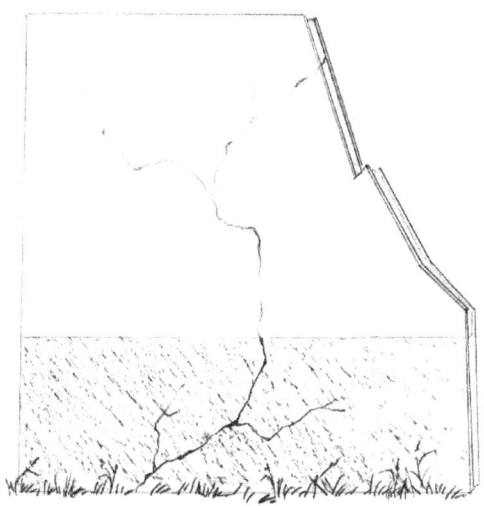

A picture might be helpful here. Think of a house where there is a crack in the foundation; it is inevitable that the crack will run up the plaster wall. You can patch the plaster all you want, but it just cracks open shortly after. To fix the problem once and for all, you have to fix the foundation. Then when you fix the plaster, it remains fixed.

We humans are not much different. We have to get back to the original injury (cracks), if we really want healing.

You will have to use your discretion here because sometimes you have to work back a step at a time, and other times you can start at the root and come forward. Prayer for help from the Holy Spirit would be useful at this point, in order to provide Knowledge and Wisdom.

A prompting that often comes to mind in counselling at this point is *'ask the Lord where you first experienced this feeling, emotion, thought, or issue'*. The source of many issues goes back to earlier life experiences, which are the foundations that we build our life upon. When the foundational experience is negative – the opposite of love, joy, peace, patience, gentleness and self-control – we then have a root that will negatively affect our life.

You can only be effective in stopping unwanted behavior, as your ability to identify and unravel the underlying structure that drives the need. In psychology there is a phrase – 'A need once fulfilled is no longer motivating'. This is why you need the Holy Spirit. To minister in this kind of prayer demands that you move in one or another of the healing gifts of the Spirit. You might refer to Appendix 'B' for an understanding of the Gifts of the Spirit. Once you, with the help of the Holy Spirit, have identified the source and root of the problem. Then you can take it to the Cross for healing.

BITTER ROOT

It seems that the channel for the Lord's healing comes to us by finding the source for the issues. Scripture puts it in a picture for us:

> See to it that no one fails to obtain the grace of God; that no root of bitterness springs up and causes trouble, and through it many become defiled.
> Hebrews 12: 15

Scripture states that the root of bitterness must not take hold; but what is the root of bitterness? It is anger, fear, not getting love the right way, loneliness, guilt, sadness, abuse, trauma, timidness, being put down, and being unaffirmed. I have found that the root can be any single event or a combination of events. When the root of bitterness takes hold, we are not experiencing the love of God and the fruit of the Spirit is not present and active. I like to say that Jesus wasn't fully able to touch this incident or event or at least not as much as He could be. Because by this bitter root, we have limited His action. When we let Him in, He transforms the bitterness to blessings.

I remember an experience that I had one day when I was walking downtown for coffee. I heard the sound of the large plastic-insert on the commercial business sign squeaking in the wind. I instantly looked over my shoulder, expecting something to happen. It was an automatic response. But why? Why did I look back?

Later in the day when I had time to reflect, I posed the question to the Lord through His Holy Spirit (Become God Focused and Identify): why did I look back? Immediately a memory came to mind. When I was just a little guy in the Okanagan fruit orchards of British Columbia, my brother, young uncle and I, were building a tree house in one of my grandfather's apple trees.

When he saw what we had done, my grandfather got quite angry and ordered us to take it down. You see, the branches of an apple tree can't handle much weight, especially the weight of a tree house. So my brother, uncle and I headed out to take it down. I stayed below, and they went up the tree and began to remove the boards and nails. When they pulled out the nails, they made a sound just like the plastic in commercial signs when the wind blows.

You can probably guess what happened! It was my job to pick up the boards that they threw down and pile them up neatly. At one point I got under the tree too early; I heard the sound of the nails just before I got hit. I was bent over when the board hit my head, and my head began to bleed. It caused quite an uproar in the family, as I remember.

So, there it is. The noise from the sign set off a negative memory with which fear and hurt was involved. It somehow resulted in an automatic behavior, where I would look over my shoulder when I heard this particular squeaking sound; there were no emotions attached, just this odd reflex behavior.

I prayed, asking the Lord into my experience (Becoming God Focused), and asked Him to take the fear and hurt away (Cleaning). I then asked that He fill it with His love and peace (Filling). I have never had a repeat experience with the squeaking sound since that day.

We must remember, however, that everything is inter-connected. Remember the spider web (Web Theory in Section I). One injury attaches to another, and each event in life is connected to the next. Therefore, problems can get quite confusing. It is important to be as specific as possible and only deal with one issue at a time.

The simplest way to deal with inter-connected issues is jot them down and then deal with one at a time.

WORKSHOP # 10

– Negative Vows or Negative Self-Talk

Some negative vows:

- I am not worthy (to be loved) – Narcissism.
- I don't trust anyone (Walls come up and relationships fail).
- I have been hurt therefore I have to control everything.
- No one will do that to me again.
- I am not okay.

Jesus puts no limit on whom He will accept, Mary Magdalene, the thief on the cross, lying, cheating, adultery, stealing – Jesus loves and invites you to turn to Him. Come to me all who are weary…

What are the Negative Vows you have made against yourself?

_____
_____
_____
_____

Take each through the *Five Fold Cycle.*

Ask the Lord into the Negative Vow (Becoming God Focused): _____
Ask the Holy Spirit for Understanding (Identify): _____
Give the Negative Vow to Jesus on the Cross (Cleansing): _____
Ask for the Lord for His Healing and Blessing (Filling): _____
Thank the Lord (Thank): _____

(c) Gifts of the Holy Spirit

Often, we need help in the identification process, as it can be confusing. We sometimes don't remember things and our mind has ways of jumbling everything up. Confusion is a very common problem.

One must remember that every experience we have is kept in the memory. In psychological studies they have touched probes in the brain, and different areas elicited different memories. They can come in color, with sound, and even smell.

It reminds me of one time when I was walking down the street, and I heard a song from my high school days; it reminded me of old memories I had forgotten. I am sure you have had a similar experience where something brought up a memory, names, faces, and experiences you had long forgotten.

CUBE THEORY

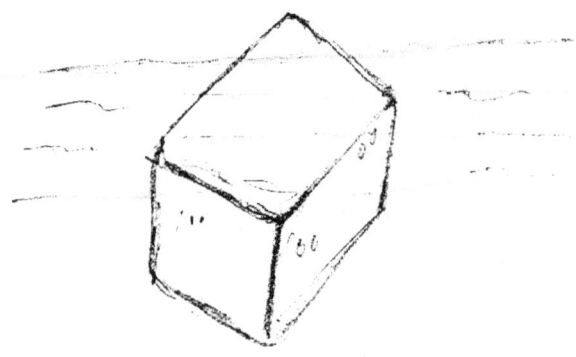

The memory is like an ice cube. Only a little of the cube is above the water line. That is the conscious memory. Below the surface is the largest part of the cube and that is our unconscious memory. It is a good image.

With this image and theory in mind it becomes obvious that we need some help from the Lord. The source of the Lord's help is His Holy Spirit, who is our Comforter, Teacher and Advocate.

SCRIPTURE ENCOUNTER – ROLES OF THE HOLY SPIRIT

TEACHER:
Luke 12: 12
[12] for the Holy Spirit will teach you at that very hour what you ought to say."

ADVOCATE:
Romans 8: 26
[26] Likewise the Spirit helps us in our weakness; for we do not know how to pray as we ought, but that very Spirit intercedes with sighs too deep for words.

John 14: 26
[26] But the Advocate, the Holy Spirit, whom the Father will send in my name, will teach you everything, and remind you of all that I have said to you.

GUIDE:
John 16: 13
[13] When the Spirit of truth comes, he will guide you into all the truth; for he will not speak on his own, but will speak whatever he hears, and he will declare to you the things that are to come.

WHAT IS YOUR UNDERSTANDING FROM THESE SCRIPTURES?

_____
_____
_____
_____

If you look at 1 Corinthians 12 - 14 it talks about the Gifts of the Holy Spirit. They are there for the asking. Appendix 'B' is meant as an introduction to the Holy Spirit and describes the Gifts.

The Gifts we need in this case are the gifts of Understanding: both Word of Knowledge and Word of Wisdom (1 Corinthians 12: 8).

Now the Lord answers prayers and he does it quite simply. You ask and then listen for a reply. The reply can come in many ways: a single word, a complete thought, a feeling, a picture or vision. The Lord can use anything and anyone. You have to be open to the Lord's Gifts. You have to listen and be attentive.

The Letter of James provides the promise; reassuring us that God will provide the information when we ask.

> If any of you is lacking in wisdom, ask God, who gives to all generously and ungrudgingly, and it will be given you.
> James 1: 5

The corollary is 'if you don't ask you don't receive'. Now that is not perfectly true, but the scripture could be written to say: 'If you don't ask you don't receive, if you don't seek you won't find and if you don't knock no one will answer the door'.

It gets to be exciting as we fine tune the Gifts and learn how the Lord speaks to us. He answers prayers!

Some books that you might enjoy in this healing prayer area are listed in the Supplemental Readings - Appendix 'D'.

(d) Problems Are Inter-Connected

There is another image you need to see to understand what happens with human problems. The image is that of a water glass with a lot of ice cubes.

WATER GLASS and CUBE THEORY

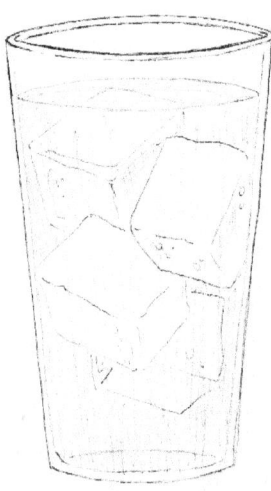

In a glass, sometimes the ice cubes bump and stick together. The same thing happens with our problems. For example, jealousy might attach to a fear you have, and as a result you have a more confusing problem.

Our job in this stage is to identify and separate the problems and issues into small manageable portions, and then take them one by one to the Lord.

Step Three: Cleaning

(a) It's Simple (as all things of God)

When we notice that something is wrong, our job is to 'do something' about it – we have to make a choice. The choice predicates an action, and the action is to bring it to the Lord and clean it up with His help.

SCRIPTURE ENCOUNTER – THERE IS NO MIDDLE GROUND

This section is meant to give you an understanding of the importance of your choices. There is no middle ground. when something twigs our conscience or when we are reminded of a negative incident, event, obstacle, issue, thought or vow. Our decision/choice must be clear. Let's look at what scriptures says:

Matthew 12: 30 – With me or against me.
[30] Whoever is not with me is against me, and whoever does not gather with me scatters.

Matthew 7: 13-14 - The gate is narrow, and the road is hard and there are few who find it.
[13] "Enter through the narrow gate; for the gate is wide and the road is easy that leads to destruction, and there are many who take it. [14] For the gate is narrow and the road is hard that leads to life, and there are few who find it.

1 John 1: 5-7 - God Is Light in Him there is no darkness.
[5] This is the message we have heard from him and proclaim to you, that God is light and in him there is no darkness at all. [6] If we say that we have fellowship with him while we are walking in darkness, we lie and do not do what is true; [7] but if we walk in the light as he himself is in the light, we have fellowship with one another, and the blood of Jesus his Son cleanses us from all sin.

John 12: 46 – Do not remain in the darkness.
[46] I have come as light into the world, so that everyone who believes in me should not remain in the darkness.

James 1: 17 – There is no shadow nor variation in the Father of lights.
[17] Every generous act of giving, with every perfect gift, is from above, coming down from the Father of lights, with whom there is no variation or shadow due to change.

2 Corinthians 6: 14 – What fellowship is there between light and darkness.
[14] Do not be mismatched with unbelievers. For what partnership is there between righteousness and lawlessness? Or what fellowship is there between light and darkness?

Luke 11: 23 – Whoever is not with me is against me.
[23] Whoever is not with me is against me, and whoever does not gather with me scatters.

Revelation 3: 15-16 – Because you are lukewarm I will spit you out of my mouth.
[15] "I know your works; you are neither cold nor hot. I wish that you were either cold or hot. [16] So, because you are lukewarm, and neither cold nor hot, I am about to spit you out of my mouth.

WHAT IS YOUR UNDERSTANDING FROM THESE SCRIPTURES?

_____
_____
_____
_____

There is no middle ground; we are not moving from negative to neutral, but rather we are moving from negative to changed, driven to go forward called to draw closer to Lord.

If we reworked the Choice line from Section I – 'An Understanding of the Background' we see that when incidents, events, obstacles, thoughts or conclusions happen in our life, we have a choice. The choice is to invite the Holy Spirit in and identify the source - root.

We are looking for the Entry Point: decision, vow, action, motivation, interest or appetite.

The counsellor's question might be *'ask the Lord where you first experienced this feeling, emotion, thought, or issue'*?

Q 10
Darkness to Light.

CHOICE LINE - REWORKED

GOD'S LIGHT

INCIDENTS or EVENTS
OBSTACLE or ISSUE
THOUGHT or VOW

CONSCIENCE / CHOICE

DARKNESS
WORLD
FLESH
OURSELVES
EVIL

Centurion in Matthew 8: 5-10 is an example of how we are to come to Jesus; humble, unworthy, expecting, trusting, inviting, and welcoming Him.

First, we bring the problem to Him in prayer. If we are at fault, we ask the Lord for forgiveness. If it is someone else's fault, we forgive them and ask the Lord to forgive them.

Forgiveness here might apply to ourselves, to others, or even to God. As a resource to understand forgiveness, I would recommend Fr. Robert DeGrandis' books[10], *Forgiveness and Inner Healing, To Forgive is Divine*, or *Brokenness to Life*.

THE ART OF FORGIVENESS

There is a difference between just forgiving and forgiving from the heart. We are reminded of Jesus on the Cross, where He had taken upon Himself all our sin. From His broken heart, He says "Forgive them, for they know not what they do" (Luke 23: 34). At the height of his physical suffering, love prevails, and He asks His Father to forgive! It seems ironical. Jesus asks his Father to forgive, but it is by His Own Sacrifice on the Cross that we are forgiven! Mary His mother, at the same time is looking up at her son with a heart pierced with a sword (Luke 2: 35).

To truly forgive from the heart is when there are no more qualifiers to our forgiveness. No more statements like 'I will forgive but never forget', 'I will forgive but I never want to see them again', or 'I will forgive but you will pay for that'. Yes, we are hurt and there is pain, but qualifiers detract from heartfelt forgiveness and indicate that more of Christ's healing is necessary. Can you meet them and say, 'I forgive them, for they know not what they do'? Can you look at the event like Mary whose heart was pierced and still exhibit love?

Forgiveness than, is opening to Christ Jesus on the cross and through Him giving our heart of love to those who have hurt us. We forgive in Him and through Him.

If we don't forgive, we block God's mercy from flowing into us – and out of us. Jesus tells us that we receive his forgiveness in the measure as we forgive the people around us.

Spiritual Law – What You Focus On Is What You Get

We must focus on eternity, think beyond our injury, and look toward the goal – you focus on salvation rather than reliving/ruminating the past. We keep our hearts free of bitterness and seeking only the goal: the promise of eternal life.

Are we the judge or is Christ? In forgiving we give/relinquish the judgement seat back to Christ Jesus and in so doing release ourselves to love more freely.

Lord, help me to be more forgiving!

The important point here is that we do whatever is necessary to clean ourselves and everyone else who comes into our minds eye.

Sometimes it helps to picture the situation in your mind and pretend that you are house cleaning. Cleaning might go like this:

- We confess our sins.
- We ask for cleansing.
- We give the problem up to the Lord, for instance, worry and anxiety.
- We ask the Lord to take away any negatives, such as anger, fear, jealousy, hurt, loss of self-esteem, loss of love, revenge, loss of memory, infantile habits, confusion, etc.
- We give up any childhood vow made in such an incident.
- Watch for decisions made which have foundations built on hurts; generally, they are always harmful. Clean them up by releasing them to the Lord.

Remember the spiritual law that applies:

Spiritual Law – Don't Hold Onto Hurts

A friend of mine, James Szilagyi, put it this way, "you either deal with it or it deals with you." Quote March 14, 2017.

Depression and neurosis are issues of our time. They are created by our interactions with the social, economic, and emotional environment in which we live. Things like love-hate relationships, sibling rivalries, unhappy marriages, conflicting loyalties, financial problems, unfulfilled ambitions, social/sexual rejection, religious guilt, etc.

Jesus has taken all our Hurts and Sickness When He Died on the Cross (Matthew 8: 17, Isaiah 53: 4).

It is often important to follow through by personal contact with the parties involved but remember to use discretion and discernment.

If you find it difficult to do this step by yourself, find a prayer partner. You might also refer to the '12 Steps' of the Alcoholics Anonymous movement. It is an excellent method of cleansing,

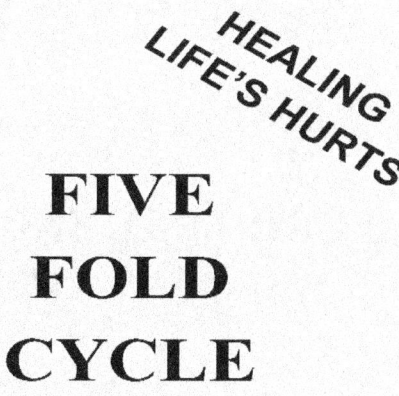

HEALING LIFE'S HURTS

FIVE FOLD CYCLE

Method of Healing Personal Hurt

... you either deal with it or it deals with you...

He took our infirmities and bore our diseases
Matthew 8: 17
NRSV

Just Try It!

FFC works...

SCRIPTURE ENCOUNTER – UNDERSTANDING FORGIVENESS

Colossians 3: 13 – Bear with one another and forgive.
^{13} Bear with one another and, if anyone has a complaint against another, forgive each other; just as the Lord has forgiven you, so you also must forgive.

Matthew 6: 14-15 – Your Father in Heaven forgives as you forgive.
^{14} For if you forgive others their trespasses, your heavenly Father will also forgive you; ^{15} but if you do not forgive others, neither will your Father forgive your trespasses.

Ephesians 1: 7 – In Jesus we have forgiveness.
^{7} In him we have redemption through his blood, the forgiveness of our trespasses, according to the riches of his grace

Luke 17: 3-4 – Repentance demands forgiveness.
^{3} Be on your guard! If another disciple sins, you must rebuke the offender, and if there is repentance, you must forgive. ^{4} And if the same person sins against you seven times a day, and turns back to you seven times and says, 'I repent,' you must forgive."

Ephesians 4: 31-32 – Put away all malice and be kind and forgive.
^{31} Put away from you all bitterness and wrath and anger and wrangling and slander, together with all malice, ^{32} and be kind to one another, tenderhearted, forgiving one another, as God in Christ has forgiven you.

1 John 1: 9 – If we confess, Jesus will forgive and cleanse us.
^{9} If we confess our sins, he who is faithful and just will forgive us our sins and cleanse us from all unrighteousness.

Matthew 6: 9-12 – The Our Father states 'Forgive as we have been forgiven'.
^{9} "Pray then in this way: Our Father in heaven, hallowed be your name. ^{10} Your kingdom come. Your will be done, on earth as it is in heaven. ^{11} Give us this day our daily bread. ^{12} And forgive us our debts, as we also have forgiven our debtors.

Mark 11: 25 – Whenever you stand praying, forgive.
[25] "Whenever you stand praying, forgive, if you have anything against anyone; so that your Father in heaven may also forgive you your trespasses."

Matthew 6: 14 – Forgiven as we forgive.
[14] For if you forgive others their trespasses, your heavenly Father will also forgive you;

Matthew 18: 21-23 – Lord, how often do I forgive?
[21] Then Peter came and said to him, "Lord, if another member of the church sins against me, how often should I forgive? As many as seven times?" [22] Jesus said to him, "Not seven times, but, I tell you, seventy-seven times.

Luke 6: 37-49 – Can we judge others?
[37] "Do not judge, and you will not be judged; do not condemn, and you will not be condemned. Forgive, and you will be forgiven; [38] give, and it will be given to you. A good measure, pressed down, shaken together, running over, will be put into your lap; for the measure you give will be the measure you get back."

Micah 7: 18 – God's Compassion and Steadfast Love.
[18] Who is a God like you, pardoning iniquity and passing over the transgression of the remnant of your possession? He does not retain his anger forever, because he delights in showing clemency.

WHAT IS YOUR UNDERSTANDING FROM THESE SCRIPTURES?

_____
_____
_____
_____

Appendix 'J' – *Practical Steps To Forgiveness*, offers a step-by-step method of applying forgiveness in your life. Give it a try.

The following Forgiveness Prayer can offer a practical way to approach God through Jesus allowing for His cleansing and pruning in our lives. It will help to open you to the Lord's forgiveness.

Prayer:

FORGIVENESS PRAYER

Lord Jesus, I want to begin today and ask for Your help, that I may forgive everyone in my life. I open myself to Your Cross, where You healed me and forgave me. I extend that forgiveness and blessing now, to everyone who has hurt me in my life.

I forgive myself for my sins, my failures and my errors. I repent Lord and ask Your forgiveness. And I thank You for that forgiveness.

I forgive my parents for their failure and their lack of attention. I forgive them for not giving me the things I needed to be healthy and whole. I forgive them for their personal failures and their lack of clear direction. I forgive them for divorce and separation. But mostly I forgive them for _____. Lord, I extend Your forgiveness to them and ask You to bless them.

Lord, I forgive my brothers and sisters who competed for our parent's love. I forgive them for hurting me and harming me. Lord, I ask You to forgive and bless my sisters and brothers.

I extend this forgiveness to the many people in my life: teachers, coaches, relatives, co-workers, friends, neighbors, clergy, employers and anyone who has hurt me in my life. I forgive them.

Especially Lord, I forgive _____, who hurt me the most. Help me Jesus to forgive them, as You forgave on the Cross.

I accept Your forgiveness and extend that forgiveness to all these people. Please bless them.

I ask these things in Your Precious Name – Jesus the Christ.

Amen.

Another important tool in cleansing is "Sacrament Confession", or "Reconciliation". You will note that it is similar to the Alcoholics Anonymous method: "Admitting to God, to ourselves, and to another human being the exact nature of our wrongs" (A.A. Step 5).

(b) Don't Dwell

It is not good to dwell on evil and the horrors of the past. This cleansing can take a moment, or it might take days of quick little prayers.

An example of how simple it can be goes like this: you are driving down the road and someone cuts you off. You immediately get angry and you raise your fist. Clearly your anger is not exhibiting God's love or God's light for that second. So what do you do? As soon as you notice the in congruence, you say:

'Lord be with me,' (Become God Focused).
'I bring this incident to you,' (Identification of the Problem).
'I am sorry for my anger, forgive me,' (Cleansing).
'Lord give me your love and your peace,' (Filling).

Then you should clean up the others hurt in the situation:

'The other driver was hurt by my anger cleanse him Lord,'
            (Cleansing and Intercessory Prayer).
'Bless him Lord' (Filling).

If your child was beside you in this incident of rage, what would have happened to them? Would they have picked up that rage? In that event the child must be cleansed of their hurt, because they would have felt that anger.

Finally, you say 'thank you Lord' (Thank you Prayer).

Now how long did that take? Two seconds. It is quite easy, as are all things of the Lord.

Authors note:

You might want to look at Appendix 'A' - *Five Fold Cycle – Method of Healing Personal Hurt* at this time. The *Five Fold Cycle* is meant as a tool you can pass on to others as part of your healing outreach. In Timothy, the Lord outlines our role as healers (1 Timothy 1: 12-17). He judged me faithful and appointed me to His service.

Just Try It!

FFC works...

Now you're cleansing could get very long if you are dealing with an abuse situation, but just be patient and do things in God's time and God's peace. There is no rush to solve all of your problems the first time you sit down.

I would challenge you that we are to expect *total* healing and wholeness in Christ. Often people are expecting instant healing, some special feeling or experience, and when this does not occur, they stop asking. You will have noticed that in this workbook we used the word *wholeness* many times. I have come to believe that "by His wounds (stripes, bruises) we are healed" (1 Peter 2: 24; Isaiah 53: 4 – 6) means what it says and we should take the attitude of St. Paul "I press on toward the goal" and "straining forward to what lies ahead" (Philippians 3: 12-14). We are challenged to keep asking until total healing is complete.

(c) Spirits and Bondage

Sometimes, however, things have gone too far, and with simple prayer you cannot get release. This is where deliverance prayer comes into play. Fr. Michael Scanlan and Randall Cirner have a good book[11] that covers this topic, called *Deliverance From Evil Spirits*. The issue in dealing with spirits and bondage, is to use the power that the Lord Jesus gave you and His apostles through his shedding of blood. You bind spirits and release or sever bondage in the name of Jesus; you then give them to Jesus to dispose of as He wishes.

(d) Thoughts Cause Feelings

This concept is important. Thoughts cause feelings; if you don't have thoughts, you don't get feelings. Of course, once the feelings start rolling you can jump all over the place, because everything is inter-connected. Remember the Spider Web Theory.

When you are identifying a problem or issue, look for a single source: is it a thought or memory? Then jot down the feelings that it emotes.

For Example: Someone Hits You

Negatives:
- I am angry
- I feel sorry for myself
- I am confused
- I want to get back
- I feel doubt
- I fantasize aggression

We clean each emotion or reaction by bringing it to the Lord, then we go on to the next thought. There is a complication here, however – emotions can attach to each other, just like problems can. You will remember the Theory of the Water Glass and Cubes. The solution is the same – divide them up and deal with them individually.

Feelings are neither right nor wrong. Take the feeling to a thought or incident. Using the *Five Fold Cycle*, reconcile yourself with your past experience – motive, feeling, etc.

THEORY OF NIBBLING THE CUBE

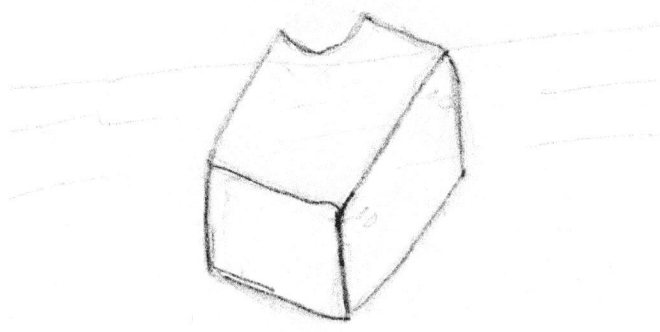

You will remember the Ice Cube Theory. If you think of fear as an ice cube, what happens when you nibble a corner of it? The ice cube rises, and other related experience comes to the surface.

Don't worry if new things rise to the conscious memory – it is normal. As you nibble away, you will get rid of the whole ice cube.

There is another Spiritual Law and Promise from the Lord:

Spiritual Law
– Problems will not be
beyond your Strength

You can trust God not to let you be tried beyond your strength, and with any trial, He will give you a way out of it, and strength to bear it (1 Corinthians 10: 13).

The Lord promises that He will keep you. All things in our testimony can be used for good, even the ugly dark stuff (Romans 8: 28).

The Cleansing Step is then simply a process of asking and seeking the Lord's help. He has assured us that if we ask, we will receive, and that we can trust in him to take us through any burden that comes our way. What a wonderful assurance.

Here is an example of how this cleaning process might go. Ron, a friend, dropped into my office one day, very upset. Ron had been studying for an insurance/mutual fund exam and said that "every time he closed the book, he could not remember anything he had studied". He said that he was "so frustrated and ready to quit".

We followed the procedure in the *Five Fold Cycle*. First we prayed, asking the Lord in and asking for His guidance (God Focused). I asked Ron to focus deeply on what he felt when he thought of his exams, and to ask for the help of the Holy Spirit to know when he had experienced that feeling before (Identify the Problem).

With only a moment of reflection, Ron remembered a time when he was a teen coming home with his report card. He found his father in the backyard and showed him the card. His father read it and stated, "you'll never make it".

Some Christian counsellors call this a curse. A father's role is to bless, lift up his child out of the mother's arms, encourage the child to stand, to walk, and to be secure and confident. This father had not blessed but put on shackles of discouragement– by saying that "you'll never make it" and that you are unable.

Ron remembers being crushed and lying against the big tree in the middle of the yard. His mind was set, his course was set, he could never succeed. He was useless!

We took these negative and false beliefs to Jesus on the cross (Cleaning). We gave them to Jesus and forgave Ron's father, and asked that his father be blessed. We asked the Lord to replace the feeling of inability with Ron's true ability (Filling). We prayed to bless his mind, his memory, and his recall under the stress of exams. We prayed to bless his ability to read, study, and remember. Ron passed the exam!

Through intercessory prayer we use the same process of cleaning to clean and heal the others in our story, in this case Ron's father.

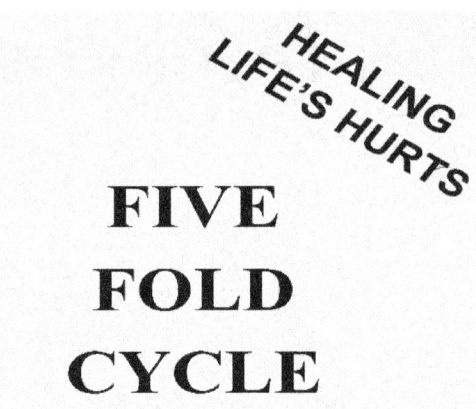

HEALING LIFE'S HURTS

FIVE FOLD CYCLE

Method of Healing Personal Hurt

... God is faithful, and he will not let you be tested beyond your strength, but with the testing he will also provide the way out so that you may be able to endure it.
1 Cor. 10:13
NRSV

Just Try It!

FFC works...

The scripture that can be applied here is from Matthew 5: 13-16 which talks about each one of us being 'Salt and Light' in the world:

[13] You are the salt of the earth; but if salt has lost its taste, how can its saltiness be restored? It is no longer good for anything, but is thrown out and trampled under foot.

[14] You are the light of the world. A city built on a hill cannot be hid. [15] No one after lighting a lamp puts it under the bushel basket, but on the lampstand, and it gives light to all in the house. [16] In the same way, let your light shine before others, so that they may see your good works and give glory to your Father in heaven.
Matthew 5: 13-16

The same promises previously mentioned (Luke 11: 9 and 1 John 5: 14-15), can be brought to bear on the lives of people around us. Like in Ron's story where we prayed for his father, it is our responsibility to be the light and the salt of the world. In this case we used a negative experience as a turning point, to pray as intercessors for Ron's father, asking forgiveness and healing to the father and the father relationship.

As we intercede for others, we spread this light and salt to the world around us. You will be surprised how your seemingly simple little prayers for people around you affect their anger, their fear, their guilt, and the like!

I remember being with a young boy who was having trouble reading the situations around him, and as a result that caused him difficulties in the playground because he hogged the ball and didn't share. We went to a mall, and I pointed out obvious problems with people around us, and then we did intercessory prayer for the situation. The idea was to teach him how to read situations and discern others.

That day there was a mother sitting in the food court with two children; she was obviously depressed. We started praying for the mother, asking that the depression be taken off her and blessing the children, who had way too much energy for someone in that condition. In just a couple minutes someone walked up to her and began to talk to her – it was like the light of God arrived. The mother's face lit up and there was a peace around her and the children. Prayer was answered!

In grief or rejoicing, fear or thanksgiving, guilt or uncertainty, we are always welcome to turn to our Father.

Who we were, does not define . . .
      who we are going to be...

Step Four: Filling

(a) It's Time To Fill

In Step 3, we talked about cleaning as if you were cleaning the house. After you are finished cleaning the problem, it is important to fill it up. It is like when you are stopping a little child from touching a hot stove – you redirect or give them something to replace that negative interest, like a sucker or toy.

In filling, we are replacing the negative things with positives, with the Lord's help. In the world of the Holy Spirit, the positives are the fruit found in Galatians:

> … the fruit of the Spirit is love, joy, peace, patience, kindness, generosity, faithfulness, gentleness, and self-control...
> Galatians 5: 22-23

There is an underlying assumption, that God wants us to be whole, integrated and healthy in Body, Mind, Soul & Spirit as expressed in Thessalonians.

> **23** May the God of peace himself sanctify you entirely; and may your spirit and soul and body be kept sound (complete) and blameless at the coming of our Lord Jesus Christ.
> 1 Thessalonians 5: 23

For example, if we have cleaned away fear, we ask the Lord for his love. If we have cleaned away guilt, we ask the Lord to replace it with good feelings about our-self.

- Doubt with assuredness and certainty.
- Confusion with understanding and confidence.
- Lack of trust with trust.
- Anger with forgiveness and love.

Just use your imagination, remembering that the Lord wants the best for us, and He wants us to be whole, for he has promised to give us all things:

> If you abide in me, and my words abide in you, ask for whatever you wish, and it will be done for you.
> John 15: 7

> O LORD my God, I cried to you for help, and you have healed me.
> Psalm 30: 2

> *Q 11*
> *Using your imagination.*

LET'S REVIEW

You are the branch attached to Jesus the vine. You gain your life's nutrients, food for your life by this relationship. Without Christ, unattached to the vine, you will wither and died. God the Father as husband/vinedresser prunes away to make us more complete, whole and sanctified in Christ Jesus.

It is a relationship. The Holy Spirit, the third person of the Trinity, resides in us, God's temple. He guides our every thought and action as we choose to open to the Spirit's action in our life.

We learn that as we 'abide in' the Spirit, our minds become one with our God and then when we ask, 'it will be done for you.' As adopted children, we gain the rights of the one who saved us. In Him is the fullness of God. This fullness is available to us.

> [9] For in Him dwells all the fullness of the Godhead bodily; [10] and you are complete in Him, who is the head of all principality and power.
> Colossians 2: 9-10 NKJV

It is quite simple how the *Five Fold Cycle – Method of Healing Personal Hurt* works. You open yourself to the Lord in prayer, you ask for the help of the Holy Spirit, and listen for directions and insights. You ask the Lord to clean the negatives away and to fill yourself and the people involved with the positives – His blessings. The Lord comes graciously blessing us, making us complete in Jesus, because all things reside in Him.

STUDY NOTES: WHAT DOES GOD CALL YOU?

Often, we are conflicted. Why would God heal me? Why would God do anything for me? I am nothing. He is the Creator. I am the created. The answer is simple as all things of God. Our God through His Scripture calls us by name:

1 John 2: 7-8 _____

1 John 3: 2 _____

1 John 4: 7 _____

3 John 1: 2 _____

I have called you by name...

Isaiah 43: 1

We are God's *beloved*; therefore, we can approach Him and He will be open to us. Who else did he call His Beloved?

[17] And a voice from heaven said, "This is my Son, the Beloved, with whom I am well pleased." Matthew 3: 17

Have you ever looked at yourself in the mirror and said, 'you are God's beloved?'

You might reflect on this quote taken from *Scripture Healing: How to ~~Play~~ Pray Scripture*:[12]

"We are created beings, each of us unique and individual. Each of us has his or her own fingerprint, his or her own iris biometric and his or her own DNA. No one will carry this uniqueness. No one will be like you."

Can you believe that fact, that you are God's beloved?[13]

At this point you might review the Study Notes from the previous page and re-consider the question: 'What does God call you?'

SCRIPTURE ENCOUNTER – POWER OF ATTORNEY

Whatever you ask in my name the Father will give you.

Scripture explains that we are given Power of Attorney, the right to act in Jesus. Power of Attorney is authorization to represent or act on another's behalf in legal matters. We are authorized to act as His agent. We have jurisdiction.

Matthew 18: 19
[19] Again, truly I tell you, if two of you agree on earth about anything you ask, it will be done for you by my Father in heaven.

Matthew 21: 22
[22] Whatever you ask for in prayer with faith, you will receive.

Mark 11: 24

²⁴ So I tell you, whatever you ask for in prayer, believe that you have received it, and it will be yours.

John 14: 13

¹³ I will do whatever you ask in my name, so that the Father may be glorified in the Son.

John 15: 7

⁷ If you abide in me, and my words abide in you, ask for whatever you wish, and it will be done for you.

John 15: 16

¹⁶ You did not choose me but I chose you. And I appointed you to go and bear fruit, fruit that will last, so that the Father will give you whatever you ask him in my name.

John 16: 23-24

²³ On that day you will ask nothing of me. Very truly, I tell you, if you ask anything of the Father in my name, he will give it to you. ²⁴ Until now you have not asked for anything in my name. Ask and you will receive, so that your joy may be complete.

James 1: 5-6

⁵ If any of you is lacking in wisdom, ask God, who gives to all generously and ungrudgingly, and it will be given you. ⁶ But ask in faith, never doubting, for the one who doubts is like a wave of the sea, driven and tossed by the wind;

WHAT IS YOUR UNDERSTANDING FROM THESE SCRIPTURES?

_____
_____
_____
_____

(b) Don't Forget The Others

When you were cleaning yourself, you also cleaned the others in the situation. So, when you fill, you need to fill the others. This is called "Intercessory Prayer". You as an intercessor; pray for their blessing, as well as your own. You will find that prayers are answered.

My brother always says that the prayer of family members is powerful. So, test this – have a child pray for a father or a husband pray for his wife. It is exciting, and the Lord will bless your prayer.

Included as Appendix 'K' is an Intercessory Prayer that you can use to pray and intercede for people. As well there are scripture arguments included for each step in the prayer. The Intercessory Prayer uses the five steps of the *Five Fold Cycle*.

(c) Asking

Underlying the filling process is the need for you to ask of the Lord. 'Ask and you will receive.' Have you noticed how many times the Lord told you to ask?

Here are a few references:
- Matthew 7: 7
- Matthew 18: 19
- Mark 11: 24
- Luke 11: 9
- John 14: 13
- John 15: 7
- James 4: 2-3
- 1 John 3: 22
- 1 John 5: 14

After that many hints, you would think we would get the message. It is like He gave us a 13th commandment: 'ask of the Lord your God, Who would love to give to you'.

In asking, we are inviting the Lord into our life. Like the prodigal son (Luke 15: 11-32) we are coming back to the source of our nourishment – the branch receiving from the vine.

Jesus is calling for persistence in our faith,
not multiplication of words but persistent ask – petition.

> **STUDY NOTES:**
> ## ABRAHAM'S FAITH
>
> **What do these lines mean to you?**
>
> Romans 4: 18-21 _____
>
> _____
>
> _____
>
> _____
>
> *Hope against hope, he believed...*
> Romans 4: 18

d) Warning

If you clean the problem or issue and do nothing to replace them with positives (blessings), there is a high probability that you can slip back into the same old routines.

One must fill the place that has been cleaned with the good things from God, through His Holy Spirit.

SCRIPTURE ENCOUNTER – WARNINGS

WARNING NOT TO LEAVE IT EMPTY:

Luke 11: 24-26 – In Luke we are warned to replace the unclean with God's blessing.
^{24} "When the unclean spirit has gone out of a person, it wanders through waterless regions looking for a resting place, but not finding any, it says, 'I will return to my house from which I came.' ^{25} When it comes, it finds it swept and put in order. ^{26} Then it goes and brings seven other spirits more evil than itself, and they enter and live there; and the last state of that person is worse than the first."

WARNING TO REPLACE THE SIN BEHAVIOR WITH GOOD BEHAVIOR:

John 5: 12-14 – Jesus warns the man not to sin any more so that nothing worse happens.
¹² They asked him, "Who is the man who said to you, 'Take it up and walk'?" ¹³ Now the man who had been healed did not know who it was, for Jesus had disappeared in the crowd that was there. ¹⁴ Later Jesus found him in the temple and said to him, "See, you have been made well! Do not sin any more, so that nothing worse happens to you."

John 8: 10-11 – Jesus warns the women caught in adultery – sin no more.
¹⁰ Jesus straightened up and said to her, "Woman, where are they? Has no one condemned you?" ¹¹ She said, "No one, sir." And Jesus said, "Neither do I condemn you. Go your way, and from now on do not sin again."

WHAT IS YOUR UNDERSTANDING FROM THESE SCRIPTURES?

_____

_____

_____

_____

In serious situations the filling process is not a one-time event. As we fill one event, our memory brings a related issue to our mind, and we continue until we are clear. When we identify serious issues or problems, we must continually fill them through prayer and scripture. I have used a system for many years called "Scripture as Medicine," a teaching from Fr. John Hampsch.[14] Because it is a very effective method, I have attached it as Appendix 'E.' It outlines how to use the promises of scripture.

If we do not fill, we will not retain the cleansing nor will we be able to resist the temptation and spiritual attacks which will bombard us in the days to follow.

We must remember we are in a spiritual battle and the only way to win is to keep our armor in good order. (Ephesians 6: 10 ff.).

(e) You And I Leak.

I like to picture myself as a human sieve – basically we all leak. Because we leak, we have to keep topping up the blessed fluid. How do we do that? We cannot get it by our efforts alone, but only by the grace of God. We must continually *ask*, we must take part in the Sacraments and attend church, we must praise and worship, and we must read the Word and apply it in our life. Communion is a "High Octane Filling Station" in the filling process. You might refer to Appendix 'L' for an explanation of Eucharist and Communion.

As we do these things, the Lord will continue to top up the blessed fluid.

A story might help to explain this idea of the Human Sieve. I remember one day when I was heading downtown to meet some friends for coffee. One of the parents from the youth group had done some t-shirt designs for me and I was carrying the designs to show folks what had been created for the youth. These were hand-made, embroidered designed t-shirts and there were just enough for each of the youth.

I entered the coffee shop and sat down with the ladies; one lady named Aleciah took one of the t-shirts to the next room to show some of her friends. When she came back, she did not have the t-shirt and told me that she had sold it. I was mad. Very mad! I grabbed the pile of samples and stormed out of the place, heading to Mass at a nearby Catholic Church.

I was on my knees praying in the church, waiting for Mass to begin, when a friend, Gerben, came up and said he saw a hole right through the middle of my back. As he touched the spot, I winced in pain – it hurt badly. I knew immediately what it was: I was angry at Aleciah and the sale of the t-shirt, and it was lodged in my back.

Now you will remember that I said we are like human sieves. I had let anger take hold and had lost the blessing; I was leaking, and I had a hole in my spiritual armor. You usually think of these holes as more symbolic, but this was a hole that when you touched it, it physically hurt – badly.

HUMAN SIEVE

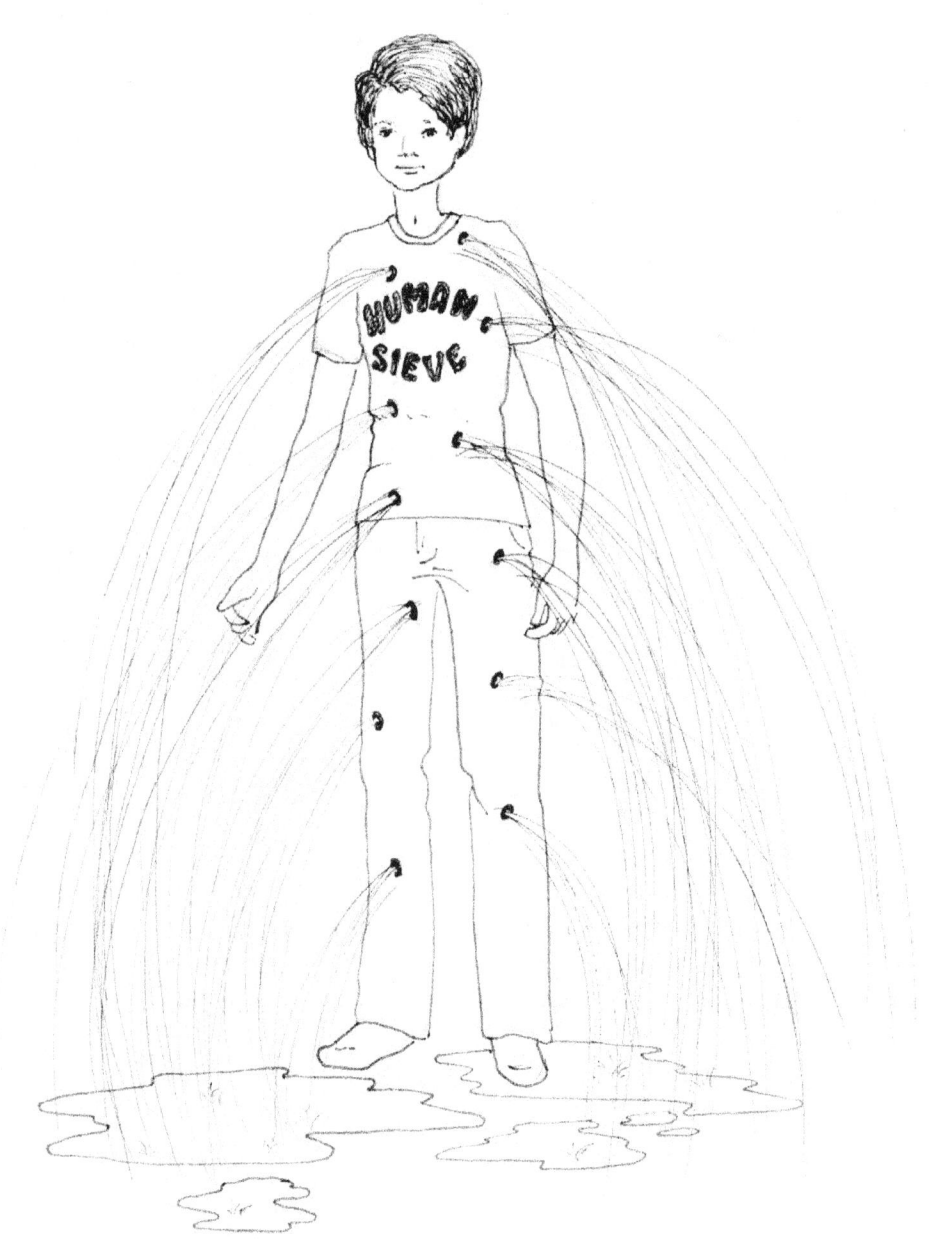

    To heal and fill it, I asked God for forgiveness, I forgave Aleciah, and then went to communion, offering up the sin (Cleaning). As I received communion, the bread of life (John 6: 32-35), I asked God to fill the spot (Filling). By the time I reached my seat, the pain had left. Just to make sure I was total healed, I asked my friend to check to see if the hole was still visible, and he said no. He has a wonderful gift, the gift of knowledge, being able to see the spiritual covering around people – you might call it an aura.

Sometimes in our negativity, we wonder if the Lord really cares. He won't necessarily calm all the storms for us, as He did for the apostles, but he can calm our troubled and anxious hearts.

We open ourselves, we trust, we let go and He honors our requests.

Step Five: Thank the Lord

Scripture has told us that when we focus on our problems, they begin to cloud us; Scripture has also told us to look away from our problems and focus on the Lord.

> Do not worry about anything, but in everything by prayer and supplication with thanksgiving let your requests be made known to God. And the peace of God, which surpasses all understanding, will guard your hearts and your minds in Christ Jesus.
> Philippians 4: 6-7

As you go through the process, you will feel and notice changes. Don't forget to thank the Lord; you thank Him in your words and your praise.

Philippians 4: 4-5 – Ask God for everything with a thankful heart.
⁴ Rejoice in the Lord always; again I will say, Rejoice. ⁵ Let your gentleness be known to everyone. The Lord is near.

The *Five Fold Cycle* has now taken us back to where we started – with God. The Five *Fold* Cycle is a systems theory[15], completed in and through the Lord. Remember the scripture which describes us as branches grafted to Jesus and the Father as the pruner and cleanser:

> I am the true vine, and my Father is the vinegrower. He removes every branch in me that bears no fruit. Every branch that bears fruit he prunes to make it bear more fruit.
> John 15: 1-2

It is a very simple process and easily fits into the ordinary methods of prayer. The process is very simple: you bring your attention to the Lord, you ask for the help of the Holy Spirit to identify the issue or problem, you clean it with the help of the Lord, you fill it with blessings from the Lord, and finally you thank the Lord.

RECAPITULATION

It is quite simple how *Five Fold Cycle – Method of Healing Personal Hurt* works. You open yourself to the Lord in prayer, you ask for the help of the Holy Spirit, and listen for directions and insights. You ask the Lord to clean the negatives away and to fill yourself and the people involved with the positives. The Lord comes through.

It all starts with a problem or issue in our life. We take that problem to the Lord in prayer, asking for help and having no idea where it would take us. The Holy Spirit guides our thoughts to a few specific situations, to specific memories. Then we pray for healing.

Healing has taught us four things: first, we are not the healer, and the gifts of the Holy Spirit are not ours. The healing comes from God through Jesus Christ, and the gifts are available to anyone who asks.

Second, God uses the community to heal. Everyone has gifts and they are for the common good. We don't own them, and we are responsible to God and the community for their proper use.

> [4] Now there are varieties of gifts, but the same Spirit; [5] and there are varieties of services, but the same Lord; [6] and there are varieties of activities, but it is the same God who activates all of them in everyone. [7] To each is given the manifestation of the Spirit for the common good.
> 1 Corinthians 12: 4-7

Thirdly, God works directly with the individual. God does not need anyone as a channel of His grace. All we need is to open to him. God can and does deal with us directly, and we do not necessarily need specialists, counsellors, healers, priests or pastors.

Fourthly, God leads if we let him. Our job is to be open, to open our will. God will then guide us and direct us, but we must be open to the promptings. God uses His people and the world around us.

STUDY NOTES:
ENCOURAGEMENT

What do these lines say about using the Spiritual Gifts?

Romans 12: 6 _____

1 Corinthians 12: 7 _____

Ephesians 4: 8, 12 _____

1 Peter 4: 10 _____

You Can Minister Spiritual Gifts...

<u>Being involved in the Healing Ministry has made three things clear:</u>

- Firstly, we are to allow the Holy Spirit to cleanse us personally, so that we can see and reflect His glory.
- Secondly, we are to see others through His eyes, (not judging others by their cover or the outside behavior), and let Him use us to help bring cleansing to others.
- Thirdly, we must not give up. Our labors are not in vain.

III. Instructions

1. When do you use This Method?

This method has been found to be useful in many areas of healing: healing of memories, healing of emotions, healing of fears and anxiety, healing the self-image, deliverance prayer, and depression, just to name a few.

Any time you are looking to receive something from the Lord you can use this method. I like to describe its use this way:

Every time you see a negative, whether in thought, memory, emotion, or happening, your job is to go to the Lord and ask for the opposite blessing. You can image it this way:

NEGATIVES TO POSITIVES

THROUGH THE CROSS

WHENEVER YOU SEE A NEGATIVE

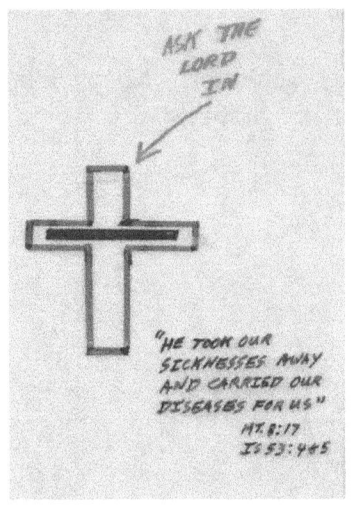

**WE BRING IT TO JESUS
THROUGH THE CROSS**

**WE ASK FOR A POSITIVE
– THE OPPOSITE GOOD THING**

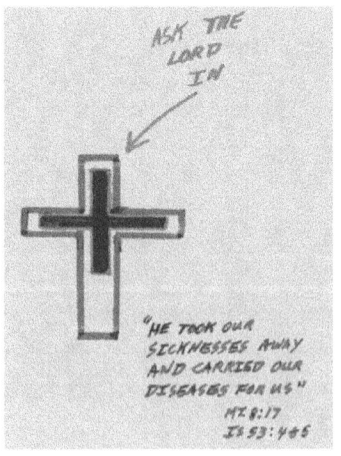

WORKSHOP # 12
– HEALING NEGATIVE THOUGHTS

Workshop: Take an inventory of the negative thoughts (Self-Talk) that percolate around in your mind and heart and their resulting feelings. Take each to the Cross and ask for the opposite good thing.

(Remember Proverbs 23: 7 – For as he thinketh in his heart, so is he: KJV)

The Apostle Paul, in Philippians 4: 8, tells us the kind of thoughts to dwell on. He says to meditate on thoughts that are:

1. true
2. honest (honorable)
3. just
4. pure
5. lovely (pleasing)
6. of good report (commendable)
7. virtuous (excellent)
8. praiseworthy

Inventory of the negative thoughts which you hold on to:

_____

_____

_____

_____

Walk the negative thoughts (Self-Talk) through the *Five Fold Cycle*:

Ask the Lord into the Negative thought (Becoming God Focused): _____
Ask the Holy Spirit for Understanding (Identify): _____
Give the Negative thought to Jesus on the Cross (Cleansing): _____
Ask for the Lord for His Healing and Blessing (Filling): _____
Thank the Lord (Thank): _____

You might look at Appendix 'C' for another explanation of Negatives to Positives through the Cross of Jesus.

2. Let's Look at Depression

In about 1985 I started training people, who said they were depressed, in *Five Fold Cycle – Method of Healing Personal Hurt*.

I learned to see depression in these terms: when we are hurt, there are three negative reactions. I learned that if I taught people to do these simple housecleaning steps, that the depression left.

There are three reactions when we get hurt: anger, guilt, and depression. Anger is outward focused, guilt is inward focused, and depression is the symptom of the two working their havoc on the person and their body.

My brother came up with the following diagram to represent the relationship between them: the two legs of the stool. He calls our anger and guilt a mushroom, or toad stool. The seat/top is contingent on the legs holding it up. The seat/top is depression.

DIAGRAM – ANGER, GUILT AND DEPRESSION

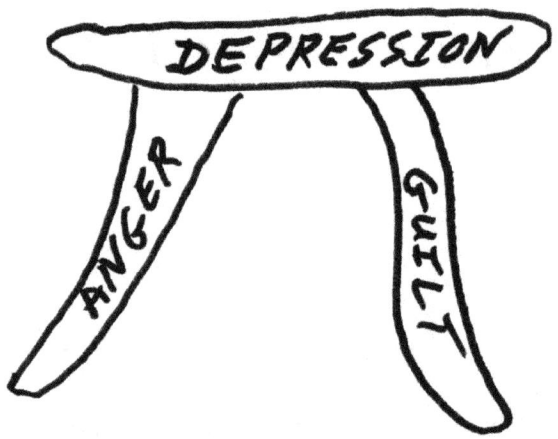

(a) ANGER

Anger is a reaction to being hurt. When we are confronted with a negative situation, we become angry, bitter, resentful, and the like. We may repress the anger and hurt, but we don't forget it. We have moved out of God's light (by choice) and moved into the darkness. We have not forgiven; our pointer finger is pointing out and we are holding someone guilty, judged. We don't let others off the hook.

External Focused Feelings

Now don't get me wrong – I am not trying to say these people who hurt us weren't wrong; I am not trying to say that the people who hurt us did not sin. The problem is that we are going against God's Law. We are taking over the role as judge and jury.

(b) GUILT

Guilt is basically taking weight onto our shoulders; it is not forgiving the self. It is worry, self-pity, uncertainty, anxiety, and tension that results from this. It is taking anger and hurt out on ourselves; the pointer finger in this case is pointing at us. We don't let ourselves off the hook.

Internal Focused Feelings

I like to think of guilt as putting on a cloak. We have the image of Joseph's cloak being the cloak of many colors; the cloak of guilt is more like a heavy weight. It blocks out God's light and it burdens us down. It presses upon us, taxes our strength, and clouds over our mind. It is evil's oppression.

Whenever we sin against someone or someone sins against us we are subjected to evil. All evil is under demonic influence which had its beginning in the fall of Adam and Eve. Even when we use an object sinfully, we subject it to demonic influence. Reality becomes disordered and we feel worthy of punishment - guilty. Contamination – we are contaminated.

We can understand the play of guilt and punishment by looking at 1 John 4:

[16] So we have known and believe the love that God has for us. God is love, and those who abide in love abide in God, and God abides in them. [17] Love has been perfected among us in this: that we may have boldness on the day of judgment, because as he is, so are we in this world. [18] There is no fear in love, but perfect love casts out fear; for fear has to do with punishment, and whoever fears has not reached perfection in love.
1 John 4: 16-18

Realizing we have violated or been violated; we feel a regret and a lessened personal worth. Guilt – a finger pointing back at self.

(c) DEPRESSION

Depression in its simplest form is the combination of anger and guilt. The two work together, spinning together to take us down and down into the depths of depression.

You can't do anything about depression because it is a symptom. You can only work on the anger, the guilt, and the unforgiveness. As you clean up each incident of unforgiveness and guilt, the depression is relieved.

The challenge then is to take each little incident or memory and work it through the *Five Fold Cycle*.[16] Each incident or memory is then used as a mini-conversion experience. We take it to the Lord, we give it to Him, we adhere to His will, and ask for His directions and blessings. Gradually, all our life comes under the Lord's scrutiny and His Healing; the Lord heals the cracks and brokenness by pruning and cleansing each little branch.

When He is finished, even our problems are transformed[17] into blessings.

FIVE FOLD CYCLE PROCESS IS SIMPLE.

No matter what the problem or need in your life, you need to open yourself to the Lord in prayer, you ask for the help of the Holy Spirit, and listen for directions and insights. You ask the Lord to clean the negatives away and to fill up yourself and other people involved with the positives. The Lord will come through. Often it is a process, but as you keep touching things in prayer they lift off and gradually complete healing occurs. Be patient and persistent. *Five Fold Cycle* works.

> *Q 12*
> *Inner Healing Prayer.*

IV. Personal Care Planning

Personal Care Planning is a tool you can use after ministry. After using the *Five Fold Cycle – Method of Healing Personal Hurt*, it is useful to review the prayer with the participants and help them plan after-care.

Often participants are overwhelmed by healing prayer. Many times they have not clearly seen the issues. Therefore, there is a need to review the prayer.

In the review, we identify the root problems and areas in the individual's life that were affected. We review the steps taken in the prayer ministry and explaining the types of prayer that was used.

Finally, we outline the need for on-going prayer, infilling and follow-up. We encourage the participant to make a commitment.

PERSONAL CARE PLANNING

ROOT PROBLEM: *In prayer to the Holy Spirit, we identify a Root Problem, (the source of the problem; the specific events or situations), and the person's response to problem. (Initial responses might include fear, anger, lust, jealousy, etc.).*

In this review, it is the time to discern what are:

- The specific problems
- The events or situations that lead to the problems
- Blocks or difficulties

It is the time to evaluate your behavior, for example fears, anger, lust, etc. What is the root cause, the entry point, the area of your life that is bound and lacking freedom?

_____

_____

_____

_____

_____

_____

BONDAGE: *Bondage (Area of your life bound by evil in some way) and manifestations (behavior reflecting lack of freedom).*

This is a summary of your findings or the Prayer Teams findings:

- What area in your life is bound by evil in some way?
- What are the manifestations, behaviors, reflecting lack of freedom?

_____
_____
_____
_____

MINISTRY: *What kind of ministry do you need: Physical Healing and blessing, Inner Healing and blessing, Repentance and Forgiveness for sinful behavior, or/and Deliverance for spiritual problem areas?*

There are 4 possible kinds of sickness with 4 corresponding prayer methods:

- **Physical Sickness** in our bodies, caused by disease/accidents & any of the other kinds of sickness, needs prayer for **Physical Healing**. Our bodies exude the residue of past hurts, accident, disease and trauma.
- **Emotional Sickness** and problems caused by the emotional hurts of our past needing **Inner Healing** prayer. This might include Healing of Memories and Emotions resulting from trauma in our life.
- **Sickness of Soul**, caused by personal sin, needs prayer for **Repentance and Forgiveness**.
- **Sickness of the Spirit** needs **Deliverance** prayer. Evil Spirits tend to attach to our woundedness and complicate healing.

What forms of prayer do you need?

_____
_____
_____
_____

PERSONAL CARE PLAN: Personal commitment and plan for on-going growth.

This step, a plan for on-going growth, is exceedingly important!

- What kind of follow-up care do you need?

- What are the practical steps need to build your life in areas which have been the object of your healing prayer?

    For example:

    - *Daily habits* like prayer, scripture & the Sacraments.
    - *Conditions* or *restrictions* on associations or habits.
    - *Accountability* - Daily phone calls or visits.
- Are there specific forms of prayer or a specific area of scripture study needed?
- Do you have a strong Christian foundation?
- Finally – set a review date.

_____
_____
_____
_____
_____
_____

My Prayer

My prayer for you is that the Lord will bless you, heal you, and bring you to wholeness as you adhere to His direction:

> You were taught to put away your former way of life, your old self, corrupt and deluded by its lusts, and to be renewed in the spirit of your minds, and to clothe yourselves with the new self, created according to the likeness of God in true righteousness and holiness.
> Ephesians 4: 22-24 and Colossians 3: 9-10

God bless you on your journey.

Ken

NOTES:

[1] HEALING PERSONAL HURT – DEFINITION / EXPLANATION
Healing Personal Hurt has been referred to by many names: "Inner Healing", "Healing of Memories" And "Healing of Emotions", "Soul Healing", "Healing Soul Wounds", "Healing Trauma", etc.
Whatever you might call it, it refers to those hurts, emotional wounds, decisions and actions that result from events in our lives such as failure, rejection, abandonment, abuse, neglect, violence, insecurity and being embarrassed, shamed, terrorized, scared, manipulated, dominated or controlled. All are emotional wounds and all are negative underlying motivations for our actions and behavior.
In Healing Personal Hurt, Jesus heals those past hurts; He transforms the memories, He removes the pain and gives us New Life. He replaces the decisions and understandings we formed in the hurt and replaces them with His Truth. Through Jesus' Cross we are healed.

[2] The Exchange is material taken form the work of Derek Prince (1915 – 2003). Materials can be obtained from Derek Prince Ministries of Canada, Box 8354, Halifax, NS, B3K 5M1, Toll Free: 1-888-737-0771.

[3] 1 Thessalonians 5: 23 refers to a division of Body, Soul and Spirit. I find it easier to understand the scripture by dividing Soul into two parts - mind and soul. I see Soul being the receptor for blessings and sin. I see mind as a separate division including thoughts, memories, will, and emotions.
Hebrews 4: 12 refers to the word of God being keener than a two edged sword cutting between Spirit and Soul.

[4] By contrast, the fruit of the Spirit is love, joy, peace, patience, kindness, generosity, faithfulness, gentleness, and self-control. There is no law against such things (Galatians 5: 22-23).

[5] Soul here is meant the receptor for the residue of sin and the receptor for grace, the result of good action and choice.

[6] Hampsch, Fr. John H. *The Touch Of The Spirit*. Fr. Hampsch (1925 – 2020) was a Claretian Missionary Priest based in Los Angeles.

[7] Fr. Robert DeGrandis (1932 – 2018) was a member of the Society of St. Joseph. He was involved in a full-time teaching, leadership training and healing ministry around the world. He was a member of the Association of Christian Therapists.

[8] Dennis (1917 – 1991) and Rita (1934 – 2021) Bennett were pioneers in the Episcopal Charismatic Renewal. Their ministry is Christian Renewal Association Inc. Rita Bennett Ministries can be reached at www.emotionallyfree.org. Please refer to Appendix 'D' for more information.

[9] *You Can Minister Spiritual Gifts* is the product of the ministry of Thomas William Roycroft (1908 – 1981), who had a powerful prophetic, healing and teaching ministry in both Southern Alberta, Canada, as well as Texas, U.S.A. The book is designed as a course to give understanding and to empower those who are seeking a relationship with God's Holy Spirit. The material will walk you through scripture and provide a strong base for your understanding of the Holy Spirit and His work in your life.

Roycroft, Thomas W. & Kenneth L. Fabbi. *You Can Minister Spiritual Gifts*, Kenneth Fabbi, Canada, 2019.

[10] Fr. Robert DeGrandis was a member of the Society of St. Joseph. Fr. DeGrandis co-authored some of the books with Betty Tapscott. Please refer to Appendix 'D' for more information.

[11] Scanlan and Cirner and other authors are listed under Deliverance in Appendix 'D'.

[12] Fabbi, Kenneth. *Scripture Healing: How to Play Pray Scripture,* Kenneth Fabbi, Canada, 2019.

[13] If you would like a good read, to open this idea of being God's beloved, I recommend Henri J.M. Nouwen's book, *Life of the Beloved: Spiritual Living in a Secular World*.

[14] Author's note: A recommended therapy is the use of Fr. John H. Hampsch's teaching on "Scripture as Medicine' found in Appendix 'E'.

[15] Author's note: Systems Theory is described as an approach to thinking that has circular causality: linear causality, openness, inter-activeness, and units that react to certain implicit rules and results.

[16] Author's Note: I recommend that you get Fr. DeGrandis' book '*Forgiveness and Inner Healing*'. Read one prayer in the morning and the other in the evening for thirty days. As you read the prayer, be attentive to problems/issues that come to your mind. These are promptings of the Holy Spirit. Take each through the *Five Fold Cycle*. FFC works – *Just Try It!*

[17] *Transforming Problems* is a book by Bert Ghezzi in the Supplemental Reading – Appendix 'D'.

[18] This is a teaching, used with permission, from the vast resource of Fr. John Hampsch, CMF, Claretian Teaching Ministry, http://catholicbooks.net.

[19] Montague, George T. *The Woman and the Way,* Servant Publications, Ann Arbor, Michigan, 1994.

[20] Anonymous. (2017, November 28). God's Temple Is In You – Meditation. *The Word Among Us*, https://wau.org.

Appendix 'A'

FIVE FOLD CYCLE – METHOD OF HEALING PERSONAL HURT
(A PROBLEM SOLVING METHOD)

I have started training people to do housecleaning. It goes like this:

When we are hurt, there are 3 negative reactions:

1. **Unforgiveness** - Anger, bitterness, resentment and the like is the first major problem.

2. **Guilt** - which is self-pity, uncertainty, not forgiving self, worry, anxiety, tension caused by worry is the second problem.

3. **Depression** - This is a symptom of the previous two and therefore when you deal with #1 and #2, depression leaves on its own.

Process:
The answer to how to deal with these is easy if you believe in Christ's help. It goes through a *Five Fold Cycle*.

1. Become God Focused: Focus on God in prayer praise and thanksgiving. Ask for the gifts of the Spirit, which include word of wisdom, word of knowledge and understanding. Be humble and penitent.

2. Identify: Identify problems and be specific. Ask for wisdom and knowledge from the Lord.
Look for specific sources for the problems and expand on them. Often problems interconnect, so make sure to separate and individualize them. Do things one at a time. It is a process of healing.

C L E A N S E

3. Clean: Do something.
   - Forgive where forgiveness is needed.
   - Forgive others, God and self
   - Bind any spiritual involvement.
   - Confess and ask for cleansing.
   - Give up the problem to the Lord, e.g.: anxiety / worry / etc.
   - Ask the Lord to take it away.
   - It is often important to actually follow through by personal contact with the parties involved. Be sensitive to the Lord's direction in this matter.
   - It is good to take these matters to the Communion Table and repeat the process.

What we are doing in this section is gradually nibbling away at the problem areas. Remember you cannot deal with depression because it is a symptom and often very global in nature.

B
L
E
S
S
I
N
G

4. Fill:
- Ask for the in-filling of the Holy Spirit.
- Ask for the contrasting good characteristics.
- Ask for the blessings and gifts to fill the space left when you cleansed yourself in # 3.
- Prayer and Scripture reading are important.
- Make sure to ask for blessings for others you have cleansed. They also need the gifts and blessings.
- Ask the Lord to heal the hurt.
- Take it to Communion or Eucharist.

If you clean the areas/problems and do nothing to replace them with positives, there is a High probability that you can slip back into the same old routines. You must fill the place that has been cleaned up, with the good things from God through his Holy Spirit.

5. Go back to # 1. Stop focusing on yourself. *Thank the Lord.*

> Appendix 'B'

THE HOLY SPIRIT AND THE GIFTS OF THE HOLY SPIRIT

To understand Inner Healing and to use it effectively, you need to use and be active in the Gifts of the Holy Spirit. Some will call it "Born of the Spirit", others "Baptized in the Spirit", but all understand that we have received an out pouring of the Holy Spirit and the Gifts have become operative in our life.

There are three relationships in God: There is a relationship with the Father, creator and first person of the Trinity. The question that I often pose is this: "Do you have a Relationship with the Father?" And the next question I ask is: "By what name does He call you?" The Father calls me Ken or Kenny, and sometimes son – special son. It is a familiar kind of call to me.

The next one looks at Jesus, the incarnate Son of God, the second person of the Blessed Trinity. The question I pose about connection to Jesus is: "Do you have a Personal Relationship with Jesus Christ?" And further I ask "by what name does He call you?" Jesus calls me friend. In my imagination we are quite close. Once in a Healing prayer about loneliness, I saw him on the back of the bicycle I was driving. His hair just flowed out to the back as we sped along the street in Medicine Hat, Alberta. I was 10 or 12 years old. Beautiful image, and in that memory there is no more loneliness!

The third person of the Trinity is the Holy Spirit. He is to dwell inside us. Our body is the temple of the Holy Spirit.

> [19] Or do you not know that your body is a temple of the Holy Spirit within you, which you have from God, and that you are not your own? [20] For you were bought with a price; therefore glorify God in your body.
> 1 Corinthians 6: 19-20

The indwelling Holy Spirit lives in us and His gifts become operative in our life. When I received the Holy Spirit at a *Life In The Spirit Seminar*, I found God became interactive in my life. I would pray and I would see His actions in my life. They came in words, in visions, by changes in my thoughts and actions, and God-incidents in my life – God became interactive.

The following page has a brief explanation of the Holy Spirit and His gifts.

What is the evidence of the Holy Spirit in your life?

UNDERSTANDING THE GIFTS

1. What is meant by Charismatic Gifts?

A charismatic gift is a manifestation of God's power and presence given freely, for God's honor and glory and for the service of others.

Specifically, the term refers to manifestations of the power of the Holy Spirit mentioned in the Scriptures, especially after Pentecost, and which have always remained with the Church in both her teaching and practice.

2. How many Charismatic Gifts are there?

Since the Charismatic Gifts are manifestations of the Holy Spirit, it is impossible to say how many there are. Scripture provides a number of lists of offices and ministries. The classical list, used by most, is St. Paul's in 1 Corinthians 12: 8-10, where nine gifts are described. These nine seem to be normal ministries that should be present in every local church.

3. Please list and describe these nine gifts.

The nine gifts, according to the usual threefold division are:

A. THE WORD GIFTS   (The Power to Say)

a) **The Gift of Tongues** -- whereby the person gives God's message, in a language unknown to him, for the community present. This Gift also includes a prayer language used for person prayer. It is a multiple gift of languages with multiple purposes.

b) **The Gift of Interpretation**-- whereby a person, after the use of the gift of tongues, gives the general meaning of what the person has said, or a response to what has been said. Interpretation can also be used privately in conjunction with the gift of prayer tongues.

c) **The Gift of Prophecy**-- whereby the person gives God's message in the vernacular for the community or for an individual.

B. THE SIGN GIFTS   (The Power To Do)

a) **The Gift of Faith**-- which enables the person at a given moment to believe, and to call upon Gods' power with a certainty that excludes all doubt.

b) **The Gift of Healing**-- which enables the person to be God's instrument in bringing about the well-being of another, on one or more levels, spiritual, psychological or physical.

c) **The Gift of Miracles**-- which enables a person to be God's instrument in either an instant healing or in some other powerful manifestation of God's power.

C. **THE INTELLECTUAL GIFTS**   (The Power to Know)

a) **The Word of Wisdom--** whereby a person is granted an insight into God's plan in a given situation and is enabled to put into words of advice or of direction.

b) **The Word of Knowledge--** whereby a person is granted an insight into a divine mystery or facet of man's relation to God and is enabled to put this into a word that helps others to grasp the mystery.

c) **The Gift of Discernment of Spirits--** whereby a person is enabled to know the source of an inspiration or action, whether it came from the Holy Spirit or from the evil spirit.

> Appendix 'C'

EVERY NEGATIVE BECOMES A POSITIVE IN THE CROSS

FIVE FOLD CYCLE – METHOD OF HEALING PERSONAL HURT

*Every time there is a negative
we take it to the Lord – asking Him in!*

1. **Become God Focused - Ask the Lord into the problem - We focus on God in prayer praise and thanksgiving.**
Ask for the gifts of the Spirit, which include wisdom, knowledge and understanding. Be penitent.

2. **Identify problems and be specific.**
Ask for wisdom and knowledge from the Lord. Look for specific sources for the problems and expand on them. (Basic problem solving method.)
   Often problems interconnect. Do things one at a time.

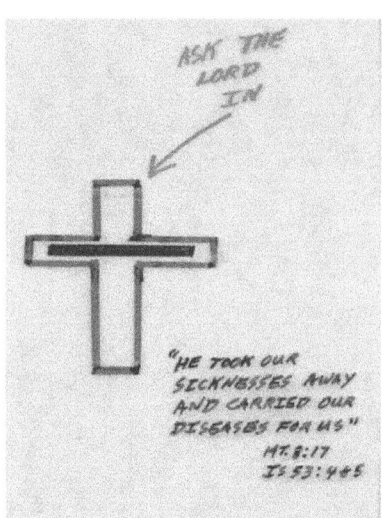

3. **Clean:**
   - Forgive where forgiveness is needed
   - Forgive others, God and self
   - Bind any spiritual involvement.
   - Confess and ask for cleansing.
   - Give up the problem to the Lord, e.g.: anxiety / worry.
   - Ask the Lord to take it away.

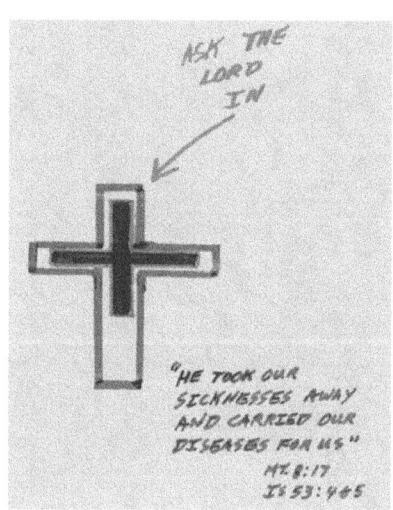

4. **Fill the empty spot with God's Blessings:**
   - Ask for the in-filling of the Holy Spirit.
   - Ask for the contrasting good characteristics.
   - Ask for the blessings and gifts to fill the space left when you cleansed yourself in # 3.
   - Prayer and Scripture reading are important.
   - Make sure to ask for blessings for others you have cleansed. They also need the gifts and blessings.
   - Ask the Lord to Heal the hurt.
   - Take it to Communion or Eucharist.

5. **Go back to # 1.** Stop focusing on yourself. *Thank the Lord.*

Appendix 'D'

SUPPLEMENTAL READINGS

1. Inner Healing References:

Bertolucci, John. *Healing: God's Work Among Us*. Ann Arbor: Servant Books, 1987.

DeGrandis, Robert. *Brokenness To Life*.

DeGrandis, Robert. *Forgiveness And Inner Healing*.

DeGrandis, Robert. *Forgiveness Is Divine*.

Ghezzi, Bert. *Transforming Problems*. Ann Arbor: Servant Books, 1986.

Green, Thomas H. *Weeds Among The Wheat*. Notre Dame: Ave Maria Press, 1984.

Hampsch, John H. *Healing Of Memories*. (Long Version), (CD) Claretian Teaching Ministry.

Linn, Matthew, and Dennis Linn, and Sheila Fabricant. *Healing The Eight Stage Of Life*. Mahwah: Paulist Press, 1965.

MacNutt, Francis. *Healing*. Notre Dame: Ave Maria Press, 1974.

Payne, Leanne. *The Broken Image: Restoring Personal Wholeness Through Healing Prayer*. Crossway Books, 1981.

Pearson, Mark A. *Christian Healing: A Practical Comprehensive Guide*. New Jersey: Chosen Books, 1990.

Sanford, Agnes. *The Healing Light*. Plainfield: Logos International, 1947.

Sandford, John Loren. *The Transformation of the Inner Man*. Tulsa: Victory House, 1982.

Sandford, Paula. *Healing Victims of Sexual Abuse*. Victory House Publishing, 1988.

Seamands, David. *Healing For Damaged Emotions*. Wheaton: Victor Books, SP Publications, Inc., 1981.

Scanlan, Michael. *Healing Principles*. Ann Arbor: Servant Books, 1987.

Shlemon, Barbara. *Healing The Hidden Self*. Notre Dame: Ave Maria Press, 1982.

Wimber, John and Kevin Spranger. *Power Healing*. New York: Row Publishers, 1987.

2. Gifts of the Holy Spirit References:

Bennett, Dennis. *Nine O'clock In The Morning*. Plainfield: Logos International, 1970.

Bennett, Dennis, et al. *The Holy Spirit And You*. Plainfield: Logos International, 1971.

DeGrandis, Robert. *Coming To New Life.*

DeGrandis, Robert. *An Introduction To The Catholic Charismatic Renewal.*

Fabbi, Kenneth L. *Powered by the Gift of Tongues*, Kenneth Fabbi, Canada, 2023.

Hampsch, John H. *The Touch Of The Spirit*. (CD) Claretian Teaching Ministry.

Roycroft, Thomas W. & Kenneth L. Fabbi. *You Can Minister Spiritual Gifts*, Kenneth Fabbi, Canada, 2019.

3. Deliverance References:

Harper, Michael. *Spiritual Warfare.* Watchung: Charisma Books, 1970.

Prince, Derek. *From Curse To Blessing: You Can Choose*. Chosen, 2006.

Prince, Derek. *Spiritual Warfare.* Whitaker House 1987.

Scanlan, Michael and Randall Cirner. *Deliverance From Evil Spirits.* Ann Arbor: Servant Books, 1980.

4. Research Review of Interaction of Religion and Health:

Koenig, McCullough, Larson. *Handbook of Religion and Health.* New York: Oxford Press, 2001.

Appendix 'E'

SCRIPTURE AS MEDICINE[18]
THE RX FROM THE DOCTOR JESUS

We often hear of people giving other people scriptures to help them through the problems they are currently facing. Maybe someone has given you a scripture. But what is the purpose of it? Why do they give each other scriptures? There must be some purpose to this act and some expectation of the one who is giving it. What is expected and what are the potential results?

So let's look at this practice in the Christian circles of giving scriptures; we will begin by looking at one of the four scriptures that give credence to this practice. In this explanation we will see how Jesus expects us to use scripture, the purpose to be accomplished, and how each one of us might use this practice.

First let's look at the scripture that gives meaning to this practice and then we will look at the Rx (prescription) from the doctor, Jesus.

Scripture: Proverbs 4: 20 – 22

[20] My child, be attentive to my words; incline your ear to my sayings.
[21] Do not let them escape from your sight; keep them within your heart.
[22] For they are life to those who find them, and healing to all their flesh.

The doctor – Jesus – gives us the prescription: a plan of action and authoritative direction for our care. Like the Rx from the Doctor.

The first lines of the scripture are directed to us personally. It says 'My son', or 'My daughter'. It is calling us in accordance to our adoptive relationship to Jesus. We are adoptive sons and daughters, heirs to the kingdom.

Jesus' first directive in verse 20 is 'be attentive'. Today one might say 'pay attention, I have something to say!' In scripture the Lord is saying *pay attention*.

Pay attention to what? The Lord is saying, 'pay attention to My words'. Jesus, the doctor, is telling us to pay attention to His words. What words and where are they? They are in the scriptures. Jesus is telling us to pay attention to His words in the scriptures.

In the next portion of verse 20, Jesus says 'incline your ear to them'. Can you see all the people with their heads bent, inclining their ears? No! It means 'hearing them': hear the scriptures.

Already you might be noting that Jesus, the doctor Jesus, is giving particular instruction. It is the Rx from the doctor. And He is discussing our different modalities.

    First: Attention   – be attentive to my words.

    Second: Hearing   – incline your ear.

    Third: Sight   – do not let them escape from your sight.

    Fourth: Heart   – keep them within your heart.

Jesus is going over four modalities, to which we must apply the scriptures. He is telling us to pay attention – keep them in our attention; always keeping them in our focus and running through our mind.

Next He is saying 'hear them'. Well to hear them, we have to say them. We know that when you are studying and you read something, if you say it and hear it, the odds are they will stay in our mind longer; Memory is increased.

Next, Jesus says 'keep them in your sight'. Put scriptures in places that you will see them. If you're a driver, put them on your dash. If you are a computer nerd, put them on the monitor. Put them on the fridge, the mirror, your T-shirt, etc. When we see them, they remind us of the message. The more often we see them, the more we remember them.

You will remember the old computer line: "Garbage In – Garbage Out". It is the same principle with attention, sight, and hearing. The more good things we put in to our minds, vision, and hearing, the more that will be stored inside and the more likely that they will be there when we need them.

Finally, Jesus says 'keep them in your heart'. What does that mean? It means to ponder on them, to stir them around inside. The heart is the storehouse of what we put into it and from it comes what is stored. Remember that the Scripture says the Virgin Mary stored these things in her heart.

Take a look at Matthew and Luke:

Matthew 12: 34 - You brood of vipers! How can you speak good things, when you are evil? For out of the abundance of the heart the mouth speaks.

Luke 6: 45 - The good person out of the good treasure of the heart produces good, and the evil person out of evil treasure produces evil; for it is out of the abundance of the heart that the mouth speaks.

Let us summarize this point:

The doctor, Jesus, is instructing us, His followers, to do four things with Scripture:

Keep them in our *Attention – Hearing – Sight –* and *Heart.*

Why? Why does He want us to keep them in our attention, hearing, sight, and heart? There is an expectation for every prescription! I refer you to verse 22 of Proverbs 4:

²² For they are life to those who find them, and healing to all their flesh.

This is the promise from Doctor Jesus. It is a twofold promise; promising life and health.

If we keep His Words in our *Attention – Hearing – Sight – and Heart,* they will give us life. Life's energy, vitality, hope, the strength to go on, etc. As well, if we keep His Words in our *Attention – Hearing – Sight – and Heart,* they will give health to our whole body.

You can understand this by looking at common issues in people's lives. If you worry you may get ulcers; if you are angry, you are more likely to have heart attacks. So, by simple logic we can know, if you hold good things in your *Attention – Hearing – Sight – and Heart,* they will cause good effects on your body. Your body defenses will be built up and be able to fight back. It's really quite simple.

The Rx from the Doctor Jesus:

Keep my Word in your *Attention – Hearing – Sight – and Heart*

The Promise:

It will give *you* life and health.

How do you apply the direction from the doctor?

It is simple, as is all things of Jesus. You take the area in your life where you are struggling, and find the scripture that speaks to it. You keep this scripture in your attention, hearing, sight, and heart. This is an example of the 'Filling' in the *Five Fold Cycle.* As you do, the problem will dissipate, life will come back to this area, and healing will occur.

My brother, Ron, used this method and taught others to use it as well. When an issue comes up, say fear, he gathers scripture relating to fear and writes them on flip cards, as you would when you are studying at school or university. He carries them in his shirt pocket. Whenever there is a free spot in the day, or an intermission in the TV program, he pulls the cards out and reads them, thinks about them, ponders them, and listens to them as he speaks them out loud. It works!

The process is simply applying scripture to the problem and letting scripture, (God's love), push the garbage out of our minds, our attention, our hearing, our sight, and our hearts.

We all know that our world has a mixture of good and bad, joy and sorrow, love and hatred. How wonderful it is to know that in the midst of all the ups and downs of life, we have one constant: almighty God loves us even more intensely as a mother loves her child.

God's love is perfect. It does not depend on what we do or how well we do it. That is because His love is based on your identity in Him: you're His child, created in His own image and likeness.

What happens when we follow the doctor's direction? We receive the fruit of our compliance. The promise, *"they are life to those who find them"* and *"health to a man's whole body."* They give healing and health throughout the body.

Here is another story to demonstrate this method of Scripture as Medicine.

And then there was John

John had these sexual ideas floating around in his head all the time. Every time there was a pause in his thinking or attention, sexual thoughts would pop into his mind. He could not stop it. John tried playing music all the time or fighting the thoughts, but sooner or later with their constant badgering, he would start giving way and would find himself in a full blown fantasy about sexual pleasures. Embarrassed and ashamed, John would come before God and beg for forgiveness, promising never to follow the thoughts again, but it just repeated and repeated as the thoughts and images took over his mind.

John knew that all his efforts and focus could not stop this spiritual assault; he said he had tried everything. So together we walked through the *Five Fold Cycle*, looking for the source and cleansing. When we came to the time for filling, it became obvious that he needed a tool to use over and over as each thought or image came into his head. Scripture, using the sword of the spirit, is a great weapon to fight and defend.

> Indeed, the word of God *is* living and active, sharper than any two-edged sword, piercing until it divides soul from spirit, joints from marrow; it *is* able to judge the thoughts and intentions of the heart.
> Hebrews 4: 12 *(Italics are put in by the author)*

So, John prayed and asked for a scripture he might use each time his mind was attacked. The scripture came quickly:

Thy word is a lamp unto my feet, and a light unto my path. - Psalm 119: 105 (KJV)

The direction for healing was that each time a thought or image came to mind, John was to say this simple psalm. John found that each time he said the psalm the ideas would disappear and gradually the thoughts and images lessened. It was a battle he won using scripture as medicine from Doctor Jesus.

Try this prescription Rx from Doctor Jesus and use 'Scripture as Medicine' in your own life!

Appendix 'F'

PRAYER FOR SALVATION

If you have never asked Jesus into your life, to be your Lord and Savior, then you should pray this prayer.

God the Father, I believe that Jesus Christ is your son and that He died for my sins. I believe He was crucified, die and on the third day Jesus rose from the dead. I ask you to forgive my sins for I am broken, and I am a sinner. I ask you Lord Jesus to come into my heart. Father, I ask you for your Holy Spirit that I might be Born Again. Father, I have Hope in Eternal Life with you in Heaven.

I proclaim your Word from Scripture to be true:

> [9] If you declare with your mouth, "Jesus is Lord," and believe in your heart that God raised him from the dead, you will be saved. [10] For it is with your heart that you believe and are justified, and it is with your mouth that you profess your faith and are saved.
> Romans 10: 9-10 (NIV)

Today I receive you Lord Jesus Christ as my personal Lord and Savior. Thank you and Amen.

"Faith is the personal relationship that comes from meeting Jesus and accepting him as our Lord and Savior. Jesus is the foundation of our entire spiritual life. 'No other foundations can be laid than the one already laid, Jesus Christ' (1 Corinthians 3: 11)."[19]

Q 13
Accepting Jesus in your heart.

RECEIVING THE HOLY SPIRIT – BAPTISM IN THE HOLY SPIRIT

Appendix 'G'

This is the Gift from God the Father that Jesus referred to in Luke 24:

> [48] You are witnesses of these things. [49] And see, I am sending upon you what my Father promised; so stay here in the city until you have been clothed with power from on high.
> Luke 24: 48-49

PRAYER FOR THE BAPTISM IN THE SPIRIT

If you have never been Baptized in the Holy Spirit you might pray these prayers.

READY YOURSELF

Take a moment to calm yourself, close your eyes, clear your mind and become quiet before the Lord.

1. PRAYER FOR EXPECTANT FAITH

LORD, GIVE ME NOW A DEEPER FAITH AND TRUST IN YOU. DEEPEN MY FAITH, LORD. HELP ME TO CLING TO YOU CLOSER THAN EVER BEFORE. I BELIEVE LORD THAT YOU LOVE ME AND WANT TO TOUCH ME.

2. PRAYER FOR REPENTANT HEART

HEAVENLY FATHER IN YOUR PRESENCE AND IN THE PRESENCE OF MY BROTHERS AND SISTERS I ACKNOWLEDGE MY SINS. I REPENT OF MY EVIL WAYS AND ASK FOR YOUR MERCY. IN THE POWER OF THE BLOOD OF JESUS PURIFY ME AND CLEANSE ME. I FIRMLY RESOLVE WITH YOUR HELP NEVER TO SIN AGAIN AND TO AVOID WHATEVER LEADS TO SIN IN THE NAME OF JESUS HAVE MERCY ON ME.

3. PRAYER FOR A FORGIVING HEART

HEAVENLY FATHER AS YOU HAVE FORGIVEN ME SO OUGHT I TO FORGIVE THOSE WHO HURT ME. FROM THE DEPTH OF MY HEART I FORGIVE AND RELEASE TO YOU_____
(This is a time to forgive and release those who have hurt you in the past. A time to open your heart to God your Father.)

4. DELIVERANCE PRAYER
(As adopted children, we receive the right to pray against evil from our Baptism.)

IN THE NAME OF JESUS, I TAKE AUTHORITY OVER ANY EVIL SPIRITS WHO MAY BE OPPRESSING ME. I BIND YOU, EVIL SPIRITS, AND I COMMAND YOU IN THE NAME OF JESUS TO BE SILENT. I SEAL YOU OFF FROM MY WOUNDEDNESS AND

HURTS AND EMOTIONS. IN THE POWER OF THE BLOOD OF JESUS, I NOW BREAK ANY SEAL YOU MAY HAVE ON ME. IN THE NAME OF JESUS, SON OF THE FATHER, SON OF THE VIRGIN MARY, I COMMAND YOU TO LEAVE NOW, AND GO TO JESUS TO BE DISPOSED OF ACCORDING TO HIS WILL.

5. PRAYER FOR HEALING

LORD JESUS, YOU ALONE KNOW THE AREAS IN MY SPIRIT THAT NEED HEALING. LET YOUR LOVE NOW FLOW IN. IN THE POWER OF YOUR PRECIOUS BLOOD HEAL ME.

6. ACCEPTING JESUS AS LORD

LORD JESUS, I ACCEPT YOU AS MY PERSONAL LORD AND SAVIOR. I PLACE YOU ON THE THRONE OF MY LIFE. I SURRENDER MY LIFE TO YOU. FROM NOW ON I BELONG TO YOU. I WANT TO WALK IN YOUR WAYS AND UNDER YOUR LORDSHIP ALL THE DAYS OF MY LIFE.

7. YIELDING TO THE BAPTISM IN THE SPIRIT

LORD, JESUS, NOW I AM READY. I HAVE EMPTIED MYSELF, REPENTED OF MY SINS, AND PROCLAIMED YOU AS MY PERSONAL LORD AND SAVIOR. I ASK YOU TO FILL ME WITH THE LIVING WATERS OF YOUR SPIRIT. I CLAIM THE PROMISE YOU MADE IF WE ASK WE WILL RECEIVE. I AM NOW ASKING LORD IN FAITH. COME HOLY SPIRIT AND BAPTIZE ME.

8. PRAYER FOR THE GIFT OF TONGUES

HOLY SPIRIT PLEASE RELEASE IN ME NOW THE GIFT OF TONGUES. I SURRENDER MY GIFT OF SPEECH TO YOU SO THAT YOU MAY ENRICH ME WITH A PERSONAL PRAYER - GIFT. HOLY SPIRIT ACCEPT THE SYLLABLES I NOW UTTER _____.

(You might focus on the Lord and repeat the word 'ABBA'.) (Often it is best to close your eyes and simply hum or sing a simple melody to the Lord, waiting on the melody to change into Tongues.)

9. PRAYER FOR THE GIFTS

HOLY SPIRIT PLEASE GIVE ME ALL THE OTHER GIFTS THAT YOU SEE FIT SO THAT I MAY BE EQUIPPED TO LEAD A FULL CHRISTIAN LIFE AND BE OF SERVICE TO THE COMMUNITY. I ASK YOU LORD TO ENRICH ME WITH THE GIFTS OF WORD OF WISDOM, WORD OF KNOWLEDGE, FAITH, HEALING, MIRACLES, PROPHECY, DISCERNMENT OF SPIRITS, PUBLIC TONGUES, AND INTERPRETATION.

10. THANKSGIVING PRAYER

THANK YOU JESUS FOR BAPTIZING ME IN YOUR HOLY SPIRIT. TO YOU BE THE GLORY.

GOD'S TEMPLE IS IN YOU - MEDITATION

The Word Among Us Meditation for November 28, 2017[20]

The days will come when there will not be left a stone upon another stone. (Luke 21:6)

People often keep postcards or photographs of vacations or dream destinations on their kitchen walls or smartphones. Why? We're trying, even if only for a moment, to experience something breathtaking, something amazing. Seeing beautiful locations takes us out of our normal lives and gives us a sense of wonder.

The Temple in Jerusalem was one such place of wonder in the ancient world. People spent their lives yearning to visit it. This was the place where God offered healing and forgiveness. Many traveled over long distances just to be there, and when they arrived, they were amazed by its beauty and grandeur. Some were even converted when they saw the greatness of God that the Temple represented, when they saw how much he wanted to dwell with his people. Although the Temple was destroyed by the Romans in AD 70, pilgrims still travel thousands of miles just to see its ruins—perhaps longing for just a glimpse of God's glory.

Where can you see the wonder of God's presence today? In yourself! You don't have to travel to Rome or Jerusalem to find God. You have received the gift of the Holy Spirit, and that makes you a temple of the Lord (1 Corinthians 6: 19)! Yes, you, with your doubts, fears, and sins. Nothing can stop God's desire to be present with you; not original sin, not the destruction of the Temple, not all the evil done by humankind, not even your own personal weaknesses. Just as God chose to be present in the ancient Temple, he chooses to be present in you.

Here's something even more wonderful: you carry God with you in the midst of your family, your co-workers, and even among strangers on the street. You might not always notice it happening, but you are the hands God uses to reach out to them in love. You are a marvel, made with more love and attention to detail than the Temple with all its costly stones. The Holy Spirit, living in you, has the power to amaze, to convert, to heal. You are much more than just a postcard. You are a temple of the living God.

"Thank you, Lord, that you are alive and active within me."

Appendix 'H'

APPENDIX 'H' - WHO AM I IN CHRIST?
IDENTITY

As a Christian we have an Identity in Christ.
The list of scriptures below describes our identity in Christ. As children of God, we are given a title and position in the Kingdom and Army of God.
Look through these scriptures and watch for the one that speaks to you. Ask for the Holy Spirit to guide you.

IDENTITY   *Finish the following line:*

In Christ I am _____

Psalm 139: 14 – I am fearfully and wonderfully made.
¹⁴I praise you, for I am fearfully and wonderfully made. Wonderful are your works; that I know very well.
Matthew 5: 13-14 – I am the salt of the earth. I am the light of the world.
¹³ "You are the salt of the earth; but if salt has lost its taste, how can its saltiness be restored? It is no longer good for anything, but is thrown out and trampled underfoot. ¹⁴ "You are the light of the world. A city built on a hill cannot be hid.
John 1: 12 – I am a child of God.
¹²But to all who received him, who believed in his name, he gave power to become children of God,
John 3: 16 – I am loved and have eternal life.
¹⁶"For God so loved the world that he gave his only Son, so that everyone who believes in him may not perish but may have eternal life.
John 15: 5 – I am part of the true vine of Christ.
⁵I am the vine, you are the branches. Those who abide in me and I in them bear much fruit, because apart from me you can do nothing.
Romans 6: 11 – I am alive to God in Christ, sin is gone.
¹¹ So you also must consider yourselves dead to sin and alive to God in Christ Jesus.
Romans 8: 17 – I am a joint heir with Christ.
¹⁷ and if children, then heirs, heirs of God and joint heirs with Christ—if, in fact, we suffer with him so that we may also be glorified with him.
1 Corinthians 6: 17 – I am united with the Lord and one spirit with Him.
¹⁷ But anyone united to the Lord becomes one spirit with him.
1 Corinthians 6: 19 – I am a temple of God, His Spirit dwell in me.
¹⁹ Or do you not know that your body is a temple of the Holy Spirit within you, which you have from God, and that you are not your own?
1 Corinthians 12: 27 – I am a member of the body of Christ.
²⁷ Now you are the body of Christ and individually members of it.
2 Corinthians 5: 17 - I am a new creation.
¹⁷ So if anyone is in Christ, there is a new creation: everything old has passed away; see, everything has become new!
2 Corinthians 5: 18-19 – I have a ministry of reconciliation.
¹⁸ All this is from God, who reconciled us to himself through Christ, and has given us the ministry of reconciliation;

2 Corinthians 5: 20 – I am an ambassador for Christ.
[20] So we are ambassadors for Christ, since God is making his appeal through us; we entreat you on behalf of Christ, be reconciled to God.

Ephesians 1: 4 – God choose me before the foundation of the world.
[4] just as he chose us in Christ before the foundation of the world to be holy and blameless before him in love.

Ephesians 2: 4-6 – I am alive in Christ and saved by His grace.
[4] But God, who is rich in mercy, out of the great love with which he loved us [5] even when we were dead through our trespasses, made us alive together with Christ—by grace you have been saved—[6] I am raised up with him and seated us with him in the heavenly places

Ephesians 2: 10 – I am God's creation created for god works.
[10] For we are what he has made us, created in Christ Jesus for good works, which God prepared beforehand to be our way of life.

Ephesians 2: 19 – I am a citizen, saint and member of god's Household.
[19] So then you are no longer strangers and aliens, but you are citizens with the saints and also members of the household of God,

Ephesians 4: 24 – I am clothed in righteousness with a new self.
[24] and to clothe yourselves with the new self, created according to the likeness of God in true righteousness and holiness.

Ephesians 6: 16 – I take the Shield of Faith to quench the evil one.
[16] With all of these, take the shield of faith, with which you will be able to quench all the flaming arrows of the evil one.

Philippians 3: 20 – I am a citizen of heaven.
[20] But our citizenship is in heaven, and it is from there that we are expecting a Savior, the Lord Jesus Christ.

Colossians 3: 12 – I am chosen, holy, beloved and clothed with compassion.
[12] As God's chosen ones, holy and beloved, clothe yourselves with compassion, kindness, humility, meekness, and patience.

1 Thessalonians 5: 5 – I am a child of the light and of the day.
[5] for you are all children of light and children of the day; we are not of the night or of darkness.

Hebrews 3: 14 – I am a partaker of Christ
[14] For we have become partners of Christ, if only we hold our first confidence firm to the end.

Galatians 3: 26 – I am a child of God.
[26] for in Christ Jesus you are all children of God through faith.

Galatians 4: 6-7 – I am both heir and son of God.
[6] And because you are children, God has sent the Spirit of his Son into our hearts, crying, "Abba! Father!" [7] So you are no longer a slave but a child, and if a child then also an heir, through God.

1 Peter 1: 16 – I am Holy because He is holy.
[16] for it is written, "You shall be holy, for I am holy."

1 Peter 1: 23 – I am born again through God's word.
[23] You have been born anew, not of perishable but of imperishable seed, through the living and enduring word of God.

1 Peter 2: 9 – I am a chosen people, a royal Priesthood & God's own.
[9] But you are a chosen race, a royal priesthood, a holy nation, God's own people, in order that you may proclaim the mighty acts of him who called you out of darkness into his marvelous light.

1 Thessalonians 1: 4 – I am chosen.
[4] For we know, brothers and sisters beloved by God, that he has chosen you,

Revelation 12: 11 – I have conquered him by the Blood of the Lamb
[11] But they have conquered him by the blood of the Lamb and by the word of their testimony, for they did not cling to life even in the face of death.

Read these statements aloud often. They will build you up.

Appendix 'I'

APPENDIX 'I' – I AM IN CHRIST THEREFORE . . .
YOUR POSITION IN CHRIST

As a Christian we have a Position in Him.
The list of scriptures below describe our position in Christ. As children of God, we are given an identity and position in the Kingdom and Army of God.
Look through these scriptures and watch for the one that speaks to you. Ask for the Holy Spirit to guide you.

POSITION *With your faith in Christ, finish this sentence:*

Therefore Since I Am In Christ ....

Isaiah 54: 14 – Because of my righteousness fear will not come near me.
[14] In righteousness you shall be established; you shall be far from oppression, for you shall not fear; and from terror, for it shall not come near you.

Mark 16: 17-18 – Miraculous signs will accompany me.
[17] And these signs will accompany those who believe: by using my name they will cast out demons; they will speak in new tongues; [18] they will pick up snakes in their hands, and if they drink any deadly thing, it will not hurt them; they will lay their hands on the sick, and they will recover."

John 15: 16 – I have been chosen to bear fruit.
[16] You did not choose me but I chose you. And I appointed you to go and bear fruit, fruit that will last, so that the Father will give you whatever you ask him in my name.

James 4: 7 – Because I submit myself to God, the devil must flee.
[7] Submit yourselves therefore to God. Resist the devil, and he will flee from you.

Romans 5: 1-2 – Since I am justified with God and stand in His glory.
[1] Therefore, since we are justified by faith, we have peace with God through our Lord Jesus Christ, [2] through whom we have obtained access to this grace in which we stand; and we boast in our hope of sharing the glory of God.

Romans 6: 6 – In Christ I am no longer a slave to sin.
[6] We know that our old self was crucified with him so that the body of sin might be destroyed, and we might no longer be enslaved to sin.

Romans 8: 1 – There is no condemnation in Christ.
[1] There is therefore now no condemnation for those who are in Christ Jesus.

Romans 8: 14-15 – I will follow the Spirit as a child of God.
[14] For all who are led by the Spirit of God are children of God. [15] For you did not receive a spirit of slavery to fall back into fear, but you have received a spirit of adoption. When we cry, "Abba! Father!"

Romans 8: 28 – We know that all things work unto good for them that love God.
[28] We know that all things work together for good for those who love God, who are called according to his purpose.

Romans 8: 37 – Because You love me I am a conqueror!
[37] No, in all these things we are more than conquerors through him who loved us.

1 Corinthians 2: 12 – With the Spirit I can understand the gifts of God.
[12] Now we have received not the spirit of the world, but the Spirit that is from God, so that we may understand the gifts bestowed on us by God.

1 Corinthians 2: 16 – I have the mind of Christ.
[16] "For who has known the mind of the Lord so as to instruct him?" But we have the mind of Christ.

2 Corinthians 1: 21-22 – God has anointed me with His seal and His Spirit.

²¹ But it is God who establishes us with you in Christ and has anointed us, ²² by putting his seal on us and giving us his Spirit in our hearts as a first installment.

Galatians 2: 20 – Christ lives in me.

²⁰ and it is no longer I who live, but it is Christ who lives in me. And the life I now live in the flesh I live by faith in the Son of God, who loved me and gave himself for me.

Galatians 3: 13 – I have been redeemed through the exchange at the Cross.

¹³ Christ redeemed us from the curse of the law by becoming a curse for us—for it is written, "Cursed is everyone who hangs on a tree"—

Ephesians 1: 3 – I am blessed with every spiritual blessing.

³ Blessed be the God and Father of our Lord Jesus Christ, who has blessed us in Christ with every spiritual blessing in the heavenly places,

Ephesians 1: 7 – In Him I am redeemed and forgiven.

⁷ In him we have redemption through his blood, the forgiveness of our trespasses, according to the riches of his grace

Ephesians 1:17-18 – I have received a spirit of wisdom and revelation, the eyes of your heart enlightened.

¹⁷ I pray that the God of our Lord Jesus Christ, the Father of glory, may give you a spirit of wisdom and revelation as you come to know him, ¹⁸ so that, with the eyes of your heart enlightened, you may know what is the hope to which he has called you, what are the riches of his glorious inheritance among the saints,

Ephesians 2: 5-6 – By grace I have been saved, raised up and seated in heaven.

⁵ even when we were dead through our trespasses, made us alive together with Christ—by grace you have been saved— ⁶ and raised us up with him and seated us with him in the heavenly places in Christ Jesus,

Ephesians 2: 8-9 – It is by grace that I have been saved.

⁸ For by grace you have been saved through faith, and this is not your own doing; it is the gift of God— ⁹ not the result of works, so that no one may boast.

Ephesians 3: 11-12 – In Christ I have access to God in boldness and confidence.

¹¹ This was in accordance with the eternal purpose that he has carried out in Christ Jesus our Lord, ¹² in whom we have access to God in boldness and confidence through faith in him.

Philippians 1: 6 – He who began a good work in me will complete it.

⁶ I am confident of this, that the one who began a good work among you will bring it to completion by the day of Jesus Christ.

Philippians 3: 14 – I press on each day toward the prize – Heaven.

¹⁴ I press on toward the goal for the prize of the heavenly call of God in Christ Jesus.

Philippians 4: 7 – The peace of God guards my heart and mind.

⁷ And the peace of God, which surpasses all understanding, will guard your hearts and your minds in Christ Jesus.

Philippians 4: 13 – I can do all things in Christ

¹³ I can do all things through him who strengthens me.

Philippians 4: 19 – God supplies all my needs according to His riches.

¹⁹ And my God will fully satisfy every need of yours according to his riches in glory in Christ Jesus.

1 John 4: 4 – The one who is in you is greater than the one who is in the world.

⁴ Little children, you are from God, and have conquered them; for the one who is in you is greater than the one who is in the world.

1 John 5: 18 – Because I am Born Again, God protects me.

¹⁸ We know that those who are born of God do not sin, but the one who was born of God protects them, and the evil one does not touch them.

Colossians 1: 13-14 – I have been rescued from the power of darkness and transfer to the kingdom.

¹³ He has rescued us from the power of darkness and transferred us into the kingdom of his beloved Son, ¹⁴ in whom we have redemption, the forgiveness of sins.

Colossians 1: 27 – Christ in me is the hope of glory.

²⁷ To them God chose to make known how great among the Gentiles are the riches of the glory of this mystery, which is Christ in you, the hope of glory.

Colossians 2: 6-7 – Christ lives in me and I am rooted and built up in Him.
⁶ As you therefore have received Christ Jesus the Lord, continue to live your lives in him, ⁷ rooted and built up in him and established in the faith, just as you were taught, abounding in thanksgiving.

Colossians 2: 9-10 – In Christ I am made full and complete.
⁹ For in him the whole fullness of deity dwells bodily, ¹⁰ and you have come to fullness in him, who is the head of every ruler and authority.

Colossians 3: 2-3 – I set my mind on heaven as I am hidden with Christ in God.
² Set your minds on things that are above, not on things that are on earth, ³ for you have died, and your life is hidden with Christ in God.

2 Timothy 1: 7 – I have been given a Spirit of power, love and self-confidence.
⁷ for God did not give us a spirit of cowardice, but rather a spirit of power and of love and of self-discipline.

2 Timothy 1: 9 – I have been called with a holy calling.
⁹ who saved us and called us with a holy calling, not according to our works but according to his own purpose and grace. This grace was given to us in Christ Jesus before the ages began,

Hebrews 2: 11 – Jesus sanctified me and calls me a brother or sister.
¹¹ For the one who sanctifies and those who are sanctified all have one Father. For this reason Jesus is not ashamed to call them brothers and sisters,

Hebrews 4: 16 – I can approach the throne of God with boldness to receive mercy.
¹⁶ Let us therefore approach the throne of grace with boldness, so that we may receive mercy and find grace to help in time of need.

1 Peter 2: 24 – He has given me righteousness and healed me.
²⁴ He himself bore our sins in his body on the cross, so that, free from sins, we might live for righteousness; by his wounds you have been healed.

2 Peter 1: 3 – He has given me everything I need.
³ His divine power has given us everything needed for life and godliness, through the knowledge of him who called us by his own glory and goodness.

Appendix 'J'

APPENDIX 'J' – PRACTICAL STEPS TO FORGIVENESS*

1) Make a decision to forgive.

- Forgiveness is not a feeling.
- Forgiveness is not an emotion.
- Forgiveness is a decision.

2) Repent and release the hurt.

- Hurt can be described as hatred, bitterness and resentment.
- These are doors to evil spirits.
- Close the doors to evil.
- Release the hurt to the Cross of Jesus

3) Forgive God, yourself and others!

4) Ask God's blessing on the other person, a blessing on yourself and a blessing on the situation.

---

*This material is taken from book by Roycroft, Thomas W. & Kenneth L. Fabbi *You Can Minister Spiritual Gifts*, Kenneth Fabbi, Canada, 2019

> Appendix 'K'

APPENDIX 'K' – INTERCESSORY PRAYER

Using the Five Fold Cycle to pray for others.

1. Become God Focused:

Lord, we know that all things are possible through you and as your children we have the right to pray for all things. I (your name) _____ bring the following people/ situation to you _____.

2. Identify:

Holy Spirit help me to understand the roots, the powers, the sin and the failure. I list the following circumstances _____, including the rebellion, the pride, the selfishness, the sin and the roots of this problem.

3. Clean:

Lord, I bring to You this situation, knowing that all things were exchanged at the Cross. I give You (people/situation) _____.
I place them on Your Cross and in Your hands. Take all their faults, their sin and their failure. I put everything on your Cross Lord.

4. Fill:

I now ask for the opposite good things to come over _____. That all the good worthy to Jesus, all the graces / blessings come upon _____, especially I ask for _____.

5. Thank You Lord:

Thank you that You have heard my prayer and that You are blessing _____.

Amen.

SCRIPTURAL ARGUMENTS FOR INTERCESSORS*

*NIV – New International Version

1. Become God Focused:

Galatians 3: 26-27 – We are Children of our good God.

²⁶ So in Christ Jesus you are all children of God through faith, ²⁷ for all of you who were baptized into Christ have clothed yourselves with Christ.

John 14: 12 – Jesus said we will do even more than He did.

¹² Very truly I tell you, whoever believes in me will do the works I have been doing, and they will do even greater things than these, because I am going to the Father.

2. Identify:

John 14: 26 – The Holy Spirit will teach us all things.

²⁶ But the Advocate, the Holy Spirit, whom the Father will send in my name, will teach you all things and will remind you of everything I have said to you.

1 Corinthians 12: 7-10 – The Holy Spirit gives us gifts.

⁷ Now to each one the manifestation of the Spirit is given for the common good. ⁸ To one there is given through the Spirit a message of wisdom, to another a message of knowledge by means of the same Spirit, ⁹ to another faith by the same Spirit, to another gifts of healing by that one Spirit, ¹⁰ to another miraculous powers, to another prophecy, to another distinguishing between spirits…

3. Clean and 4. Fill:

Isaiah 53: 4-6 – There was an exchange at the Cross.

⁴ Surely he took up our pain and bore our suffering, yet we considered him punished by God, stricken by him, and afflicted. ⁵ But he was pierced for our transgressions, he was crushed for our iniquities; the punishment that brought us peace was on him, and by his wounds we are healed. ⁶ We all, like sheep, have gone astray, each of us has turned to our own way; and the LORD has laid on him the iniquity of us all.

5. Thank You Lord:

1 Thessalonians 5: 18 – Give thanks to God in all things.

¹⁸ give thanks in all circumstances; for this is God's will for you in Christ Jesus.

Appendix 'L'

HEALING THROUGH COMMUNION

In the *Five Fold Cycle*[I], I have mentioned Communion as a high-octane source of healing. I have referred to it at least 6 times in the material, especially in the *Filling* stage where we are seeking God's touch in our life through the Cross of Jesus.

One might wonder about these comments and it opens the reader to speculation. Let me flush out this idea.

If you remember, the story of Kora Lynne one fact that is missing in the story was my direction to her to receive Communion every day. In fact, each time she visited my office we would walk down to the Church and receive Communion as a balm in the healing. We took each thing we found in the prayer time and brought it to the Communion Table, giving it to Christ and asking for the blessing due to Him.

How might we understand this direction to Kora Lynne?

First, it is a 'participation':

> [17] *Because there is one loaf, we, who are many, are one body, for we all share the one loaf.*
> 1 Corinthians 10: 17 NIV

"We are partakers of the only source of Life: the body and the blood of the Lord." As partakers, we become one with the Lord. One Body in Christ.

Second, we receive 'Life':

> [53] *Jesus said to them, "Very truly I tell you, unless you eat the flesh of the Son of Man and drink his blood, you have no life in you.* [54] *Whoever eats my flesh and drinks my blood has eternal life, and I will raise them up at the last day.* [55] *For my flesh is real food and my blood is real drink.* [56] *Whoever eats my flesh and drinks my blood remains in me, and I in them.* [57] *Just as the living Father sent me and I live because of the Father, so the one who feeds on me will live because of me.* [58] *This is the bread that came down from heaven. Your ancestors ate manna and died, but whoever feeds on this bread will live forever."*
> John 6: 53–58

The scripture states 'unless we partake of this flesh and blood there is no life in us'. God gives life to the Son; the Son is the life source of the believer. When we partake of communion, we partake of the source of life.

The Exchange:[II]

As believers, we accept that Jesus took away our sin at the exchange on the Cross.

> *²¹ God made him who had no sin to be sin[a] for us, so that in him we might become the righteousness of God.*
> 2 Corinthians 5: 21
> [a] Sin here could be rebellion.

But there is more, much more. At the Cross of Jesus there was an exchange for any need or problem in our life. God the Father, through Jesus passion and death, provides provision or His solution. And that one place is the Cross of Jesus. This provision is for everything; spiritual, physical, material, for time or eternity.

This is expressed in a number of scriptures:

> *²⁴ "He himself bore our sins" in his body on the cross, so that we might die to sins and live for righteousness; "by his wounds you have been healed."*
> 1 Peter 2: 24

> *⁴ Surely he took up our pain and bore our suffering, yet we considered him punished by God, stricken by him, and afflicted.*
> *⁵ But he was pierced for our transgressions, he was crushed for our iniquities; the punishment that brought us peace was on him, and by his wounds we are healed.*
> Isaiah 53: 4-6

God laid on Jesus the iniquity of us all. That is the negative part of the exchange. The positive side is that in return, all the good that was due to the sinless obedience of Jesus is available to us. God visited upon Jesus the evil due to us that in return He might make available to us the good due to Jesus.

Healing here means physical, psychological, emotional, spiritual and more – all our needs. The scripture is written in the past tense – are healed and have been healed.

When I send someone to Communion, I expecting that our good God through His Son will complete the work we have presented in prayer. And He does!

Examples of Bread filling and nurturing those in Scripture:

In 1 Kings 19: 4-8 an angel appears to Elijah and tells him, "Get up and eat, otherwise the journey will be too much for you." Elijah wakes to find a stone cooked loaf in front of him. He is woken twice and told to eat, that this will give him the nourishment that he needs to walk the 40 days.

In the gospel John 6: 41-51 we are reminded that Jesus is the bread of life and we need to be fed by Him or the journey will be too much for us. The Israelites ate manna, physical food, in the dessert (Exodus 16) for forty years, until they came to the Promised Land; they ate manna until they reached the border of Canaan.

We call these a 'Type' in that they are a foreshadow of what will be. Manna foreshadows the bread Jesus offers at the Last Supper and which is repeated at the Communion Table.
Eucharist is a *spiritual food*, offered to us to help us on the journey of life. It is meant to keep us strong during the times of trial, despair, doubt, worry, confusion, all of which is better known as 'life'. God offers us 'the bread of life' to sustain us on the journey.

In Kora Lynne's story not told in the book, she regularly came to the Communion Table, put her hand out with all the issues that had troubled her and caused her trauma, then received the bread and wine as a healing balm. When she returned to her seat she would open to what the Lord was doing in her life, and how He was healing those hurts and traumas from the past. In the act, she gave the issues to the Cross and received the blessing and healing from Jesus the Bread of Life, becoming renewed and whole in mind, body soul and spirit.

Jesus is the Bread of Life:

In John 6 there is a discourse between Jesus and crowd at Capernaum. Jesus has told them in verse 29 that they are to believe in the one God the Father has sent and the crowd is muttering that He must show them a sign.

> *30 So they asked him, "What sign then will you give that we may see it and believe you? What will you do? 31 Our ancestors ate the manna in the wilderness; as it is written: 'He gave them bread from heaven to eat.'"*[III]
> John 6: 30-31 NIV

Jesus then refers them to history where the miracle of the manna, falling from Heaven, feeds the starving people on the Exodus.

> *32 Jesus said to them, "Very truly I tell you, it is not Moses who has given you the bread from heaven, but it is my Father who gives you the true bread from heaven. 33 For the bread of God is the bread that comes down from heaven and gives life to the world."*
> John 6: 32-33 NIV

The people respond by asking Jesus for this bread always to be available and Jesus responds.

> *34 "Sir," they said, "always give us this bread." 35 Then Jesus declared, "I am the bread of life. Whoever comes to me will never go hungry, and whoever believes in me will never be thirsty.*
> John 6: 34-35 NIV

There was more murmuring and Jesus responds.

> *48 I am the bread of life. 49 Your ancestors ate the manna in the wilderness, yet they died. 50 But here is the bread that comes down from heaven, which anyone may eat and not die. 51 I am the living bread that came down from heaven. Whoever eats this bread will live forever. This bread is my flesh, which I will give for the life of the world."*
> John 6: 48-51 NIV

It must have been hard for Jesus to hear but the crowd began to argue about eating His flesh like cannibals. Now this is Jesus speaking and He would have known that they were confused and did not understand Him clearly. He could have said, no I was talking figuratively and it has to do only with belief in me in your hearts or in your mind. But He did not. He could have refuted to idea of eating him like a cannibal but He did not. And once again Jesus does not back down. He referred them once again to the manna experience of the Exodus.

⁵² Then the Jews began to argue sharply among themselves, "How can this man give us his flesh to eat?" ⁵³ Jesus said to them, "Very truly I tell you, unless you eat the flesh of the Son of Man and drink his blood, you have no life in you. ⁵⁴ Whoever eats my flesh and drinks my blood has eternal life, and I will raise them up at the last day. ⁵⁵ For my flesh is real food and my blood is real drink. ⁵⁶ Whoever eats my flesh and drinks my blood remains in me, and I in them. ⁵⁷ Just as the living Father sent me and I live because of the Father, so the one who feeds on me will live because of me. ⁵⁸ This is the bread that came down from heaven. Your ancestors ate manna and died, but whoever feeds on this bread will live forever." ⁵⁹ He said this while teaching in the synagogue in Capernaum.
John 6: 52-59 NIV

Jesus then heard His disciples questioning and again He answers by referring them to what will come, His death and resurrection. He is telling them to think outside the box. That this God's Son speaking and that He brings New Life in new ways.

⁶⁰ On hearing it, many of his disciples said, "This is a hard teaching. Who can accept it?" ⁶¹ Aware that his disciples were grumbling about this, Jesus said to them, "Does this offend you? ⁶² Then what if you see the Son of Man ascend to where he was before! ⁶³ The Spirit gives life; the flesh counts for nothing. The words I have spoken to you—they are Spirit and life. ⁶⁴ Yet there are some of you who do not believe." For Jesus had known from the beginning which of them did not believe and who would betray him.
John 6: 60-64 NIV

Jesus is clearly pointing to the future. In the Bread of Life discourse, He points to the Communion table just as He points to His Death and Resurrection.

Institution of the Eucharist – Communion Table:

There are four accounts of the institution of the Eucharist. The earliest is that of Paul 1 Corinthians 11: 23-26. The others are Mark 14: 22-24; Matthew 26: 26-30; and Luke 22:14-23.

In my counselling work I found that taking people or directing people to the Eucharist or Communion Table brought a level of healing that was deep and powerful, that this sacrifice offered by Jesus was the basis of the Exchange – Blood Offering. That sacrifice was the foundation of healing and wholeness in Christ.

In Summary:
I have mentioned Communion as a high-octane source of healing. I encourage those receiving Healing Prayer, Inner Healing, Healing of Emotions and Memories and these forms of Healing Life's Hurts to take what they have prayed to the Communion Table. Once again presenting it to the Lord at this Sacrifice where He exchanged His Blessing for our brokenness.

We see this reception of bread as being nurturing for our needs both in the Manna that nourished the Israelites and where Elijah wakes to find a stone cooked loaf in front of him. Eucharist is a *spiritual food*, offered to us to help us on the journey of life.

Jesus is the Bread of Life and Jesus declared, *"I am the bread of life. Whoever comes to me will never go hungry, and whoever believes in me will never be thirsty."* Jesus is clearly pointing to the future. In the Bread of Life discourse, He points to the Communion table just as He points to His Death and Resurrection.

My encouragement is that you take your brokenness and review your prayer for healing at the Communion Table. It is a feeding station – the source of Spiritual Food.

[I] Five Fold Cycle – Method of Healing Personal Hurt.
[II] You might look at material describing the Exchange in Section I. 2. *What do we do to Break out of This Cycle?*
[III] John 6: 31 refers to *"Our ancestors ate the manna in the wilderness"* – references include: Exodus 16: 4; Nehemiah 9: 15; Psalm 78: 24, 25.

ANSWERS TO STUDY NOTES

STUDY NOTES: **Page 5**
WHAT DO YOU LEARN FROM EACH SCRIPTURE?

Exodus 20: 4-5	Punishment for idols to the third and fourth generation.
Exodus 34: 6-7	The Lord keeps his love to the 1000th generation.
Leviticus 26: 40-42	I will remember my covenants with Jacob, Isaac and Abraham and the land.
Deuteronomy 5: 9-10	Punishment for the third and fourth generation and blessing to the thousandth.
Deuteronomy 7: 9-11	Blessings to the thousandth generation.
Jeremiah 32: 18	Blessing to the thousandth generation.

STUDY NOTES: Page 11
THE EXCHANGE

What was exchanged?

Galatians 3: 13-14	Jesus becomes a curse, that we might receive the blessing
1 Peter 2: 24	By His wounds we are healed.
Matthew 8: 17	He took our infirmities and bore our diseases.
2 Corinthians 5: 21	Jesus is made sin, so that we receive righteousness.
Hebrews 2: 9	He suffers death, that we might receive life.
Isaiah 53: 4-6	All our inequity is laid on Him, that we might be whole.
Hebrews 9: 15	He is the Mediator of a New Covenant that we may receive eternal life
Hebrews 9: 24-28	By His Sacrifice He removed sin once for all
Hebrews 10: 10	By the offering of His body, we have been sanctified once for all.
Romans 6: 23	Jesus was punished that we might be forgiven.
2 Corinthians 8: 9	Jesus took our poverty that we might share His abundance.
Matthew 27: 46	Jesus was rejected by God the Father that we might have acceptance.

Christ is the mediator of a new covenant - once and for all!
1 Timothy 2: 5

STUDY NOTES: Page 16
NOT MY WILL BUT YOURS BE DONE

Review these scriptures. What do they say to you?

Matthew 26: 39   "…let this cup pass from me; yet not what I want but what you want."

Luke 22: 42   "Father, if you are willing, remove this cup from me; yet, not my will but yours be done."

Mark 14: 36   "Abba, Father, for you all things are possible; remove this cup from me; yet, not what I want, but what you want."

John 6: 38   I have come down from heaven, not to do my own will, but the will of him who sent me.

I am the vine, you are the branches. Those who abide in me and I in them
bear much fruit, because apart from me you can do nothing.
John 15: 5

STUDY NOTES: Page 24
COLLABORATE WITH HOLY SPIRIT

Review these scriptures. What do they say to you?

Luke 9: 23   Deny yourself.

Galatians 5: 24-25   Crucify your flesh with its passions and desires. Collaborate with the Spirit.

2 Corinthians 5: 17   Old has passed away. We are a new creation.

Ephesians 4: 22-24   Lay aside your old self and put on a new self.

Now the Lord is the Spirit, and where the Spirit of the Lord is, there is freedom.
2 Corinthians 3:17

STUDY NOTES: Page 33
WE ARE SPIRIT FIRST

What do these lines mean to you?

Jeremiah 1: 5	God knew us before we were born
Psalm 139: 13 & Jeremiah 1: 5	He fashioned us in our mother's womb
1 Corinthians 3: 16 & 2 Corinthians 1: 22	He put His Spirit in us.
Genesis 1: 27	We are made in His likeness.

For in him we live, and move, and have our being. . . Acts 17:28

STUDY NOTES: WHAT DOES GOD CALL YOU?

Often we are conflicted. Why would God heal me? Why would God do anything for me? I am nothing. He is the Creator. I am the created. The answer is simple as all things of God. Our God through His Scripture calls us by name:

1 John 2: 7-8

[7] Beloved, I am writing you no new commandment, but an old commandment that you have had from the beginning; the old commandment is the word that you have heard. [8] Yet I am writing you a new commandment that is true in him and in you, because the darkness is passing away and the true light is already shining.

1 John 3: 2

[2] Beloved, we are God's children now; what we will be has not yet been revealed. What we do know is this: when he is revealed, we will be like him, for we will see him as he is.

1 John 4: 7

[7] Beloved, let us love one another, because love is from God; everyone who loves is born of God and knows God.

3 John 1: 2

[2] Beloved, I pray that all may go well with you and that you may be in good health, just as it is well with your soul

---

I have called you by name…
Isaiah 43: 1

STUDY NOTES: Page 73
ABRAHAM'S FAITH

What do these lines mean to you?

Romans 4: 18-21 – Since God had promised it, Abraham believed convinced that God was able to do what He had promised.

[18] Hoping against hope, he believed that he would become "the father of many nations," according to what was said, "So numerous shall your descendants be." [19] He did not weaken in faith when he considered his own body, which was already as good as dead (for he was about a hundred years old), or when he considered the barrenness of Sarah's womb. [20] No distrust made him waver concerning the promise of God, but he grew strong in his faith as he gave glory to God, [21] being fully convinced that God was able to do what he had promised.

Hope against hope, he believed...
Romans 4: 18

STUDY NOTES: Page 78
ENCOURAGEMENT

What do these lines say about using the Spiritual Gifts?

God has given the Church various gifts in order to help us minister effectively. He has scattered encouragement in several places in the New Testament. Here are a few:

Romans 12: 6 – Gift differ according to the grace given to us,

> [6] We have gifts that differ according to the grace given to us . . .

1 Corinthians 12: 7 – To each is given the manifestation of the Holy Spirit for the common good.

> [7] To each is given the manifestation of the Spirit for the common good.

Ephesians 4: 8, 12 – Jesus gave men gifts to equip the saints and build the body.

> [8] Therefore it is said, "When he ascended on high he made captivity itself a captive; he gave gifts to his people."
> [12] to equip the saints for the work of ministry, for building up the body of Christ,

1 Peter 4: 10 – Each has received a gift, employ it for one another.

> [10] Like good stewards of the manifold grace of God, serve one another with whatever gift each of you has received.

You Can Minister Spiritual Gifts…

FAQ – QUESTIONS OFFER A DEEPER UNDERSTANDING:

As people worked through the *Five Fold Cycle – Method of Healing Personal Hurt,* they have asked questions. Often these were blocks to their understanding. The answers that follow offer underlying ideas and concepts.

I want to thank those who asked the questions. It is my hope that through the explanation's others will glean deeper understanding of the Lord's healing.

Q 1
Born Again.

– BORN AGAIN (Re-Created – New Life) – Page 19

What is this Born Again? I find it quite confusing. When I was baptized and confirmed I did not see any difference. Could you explain this re-creation, this New Life?

Being Born Again is hard to fathom, but when we join the Lord Jesus, we become adopted children. Through this adoption we gain the privileges of sons and daughters. Let me explain.

At baptism God breathes His Holy Spirit into us. He makes us a new creation.

> *So if anyone is in Christ, there is a new creation: everything old has passed away; look, new things have come into being!*
> 2 Corinthians 5: 17

God also begins a process of renovation within us. For the rest of our lives, God works at changing us from the inside out. We are to become images of His Son.

Second, as children of God, we have a new connection with God. With His indwelling Holy Spirit, we come into relationship with our Father. We are no longer under fear of striving to win His affection. In our woundedness we often look to fill this void by looking for love in all the wrong places. This new relationship with the Father gives us inner faith and hope. It is a relationship of love, peace, and security. We are drawn to Him with love and gratitude. We don't need to do anything for Him - He loves us, no matter what.

These new inner motivations drive us to humbly obey Him. When we fall, we feel safe to stand up again, knowing He will always take us back. There is repentance and forgiveness.

Thirdly, we are God's beloved. He loves us like His son.

> *And a voice came from the heavens, "You are my Son, the Beloved; with you I am well pleased."*
> Mark 1: 11

God looks at us like His son. We are His beloved. God created us in His image.

It is amazing! God Our Father has called us. He has made us in His image. As His beloved, He gives us His Holy Spirit, who resides within us and works on us to be holy as He is Holy.

Q 2 — NEED TO HEAL THE BODY – Page 20

Need to Heal the Body.

You mention the need to heal the Body. You often mention in your presentations that the body is a collector of personal hurts and is like a tuning-fork. Could you explain what you mean in reference to the need to heal the body?

Good question. When we are hurt though trauma, accident or negative interpersonal dynamics, we often dump the residue on our body. For example, we know that Type A individuals are outgoing, ambitious, rigidly organized, highly status-conscious, impatient, anxious, proactive, and concerned with time management. People with Type A personalities are often high-achieving "workaholics". Because of this, Type A personalities appear to have higher rates of obesity, high blood pressure, heart disease and stroke.

With that example in mind, we realize that the body is affected by our behavior, decisions and the circumstances of our life. In healing prayer when we look to heal personal hurt, we must look at both the root of the problem and where the body has stored the hurt. We are looking for 'wholeness.'

The image of a tuning-fork helps us see that the body, like a tuning-fork, picks up the vibrations around it – vibrations might be thought of as life's traumas or experiences. We want the body to be covered by the whole armor of God, be sound, and complete. You might ask the question, "where do I store negative energy in my body?" Examples of these places might be the migraine headache, the achy jaw, the heart pains, the stomachaches, the sore shoulder, etc.

Scripture describes wholeness as a body that is sound (complete KJV, blameless NIV, whole and undamaged AMP):

> [23] May the God of peace himself sanctify you entirely; and may your spirit and soul and body be kept sound (complete) and blameless at the coming of our Lord Jesus Christ.
> 1 Thessalonians 5: 23

And we know that Jesus bore our sins in His body on the Cross:

> He himself bore our sins in his body on the cross, so that, free from sins, we might live for righteousness; by his wounds you have been healed.
> 1 Peter 2: 24; Isaiah 53: 4 – 6

Through Inner Healing prayer we look at the four areas Body, Mind, Soul and Spirit with the desire that they become sound, whole, unified and complete.

When dealing with the memory you might consider that there are three places in the body where memory is stored: mind, heart and gut. Where do you store your negative memory? Pray to bring God's healing into that area of your body.

We are looking for the body point – place where we store negative energy. When we identify the body point, we invite the Holy Spirit to heal us, releasing the negative to the Cross of Jesus, applying the Exchange at the Cross.

Q 3
The Spirit.

– THE SPIRIT - Page 25

In your books you put a lot of emphasis on the Holy Spirit. Why don't you just pray to Jesus?

Each of the three persons, although one God, has a role in the healing process. The Father is Creator and has creative powers. Jesus the Son is the savior who took on himself all our 'wounds.' If we have a need or problem in our life, there is only one place and one place alone where you must go to find the provision or God's solution. Through His passion and suffering we were made whole.

> But he was wounded for our transgressions, crushed for our iniquities; upon him was the punishment that made us whole, and by his bruises we are healed.
> Isaiah 53: 5

The Holy Spirit is the conduit to Father and Son. The Spirit gives us Gifts allowing us to access all understanding. Through the Gifts of Word of Knowledge, Word of Wisdom and Discernment of Spirits we are able to source the Root of our problems.

Jesus promises the Holy Spirit who will reside within us

> [15] If you love me, you will keep my commandments. [16] And I will ask the Father, and he will give you another Advocate, to be with you forever. [17] This is the Spirit of truth, whom the world cannot receive, because it neither sees him nor knows him. You know him, because he abides with you, and he will be in you.
> John 14: 15-17 NRSV

The Holy Spirit, the Advocate will teach us all things and remind us of Jesus words.

> [26] But the Advocate, the Holy Spirit, whom the Father will send in my name, will teach you all things and will remind you of everything I have said to you.

John 14: 26 NRSV

As a result of this closer intimacy the Holy Spirit begins what I call "house cleaning"— He reveals to us those things in our lives that are not pleasing to God. He takes away our desire to do the things we did before that were displeasing to Him and gives us the power to resist temptations. This is life-changing in every respect.

You can see an ultimate plan in process, The Father first sends Jesus to make us right – righteous. Next the Father sends the Holy Spirit to guide, teach and heal. All of this to help us come closer to Him.

> *Q 4*
> *Baptism in the Spirit*

– BAPTISM IN THE SPIRIT - Page 26

What is Baptism In The Spirit? Is it different than Baptism or what they call Confirmation in the mainline churches?

Baptism of the Holy Spirit comes when the Holy Spirit, already residing in us from the time we accepted Jesus as Savior, is released to operate fully in our lives. As Dennis Bennett used to say, the question is not, "Do you have the Holy Spirit?" But rather, "Does the Holy Spirit have you?"

From the day of His conception, the Holy Spirit resided in Jesus. There was never a moment in His life when He was not God. Yet, for the first 30 years of His life, there is no recorded ministry of Jesus, other than those occasions when He was found in the temple as a young boy. Except for the wedding feast at Cana (John 2: 1-12), there are no recorded teachings or miracles — not until He was baptized in the Jordan at the hands of John the Baptist. This was the event in Jesus' life where the Holy Spirit was released to empower His ministry.

So, what happened to Him at the River Jordan? John says Jesus was baptized in the Holy Spirit.

> [32] And John testified, 'I saw the Spirit descending from heaven like a dove, and it remained on him.
> John 1: 32

His disciples also had an experience at Pentecost (Acts 2: 1-4), where they were empowerment by the Holy Spirit to heal, teach and lead people to a closer relationship with God.

When the Holy Spirit is released in our lives, we discover it is possible to live the way God expects us to live, and His power affects every area of our lives. Listening to God's Spirit is essential for healing.

Must everyone be baptized in the Holy Spirit? Jesus said,

¹³ If you then, who are evil, know how to give good gifts to your children, how much more will the heavenly Father give the Holy Spirit to those who ask him!'
Luke 11: 13

From this we understand that the Holy Spirit is available to everyone.

The Baptism in the Spirit is a release of the Spirit, usually occurring with the realization that there is a potential available that we have not activated. People may well have been Baptised and received Confirmation but never enter into an inter-active relationship with the Holy Spirit. It is like receiving a wrapped gift and putting it on the mantle. You have received it, but you have not opened the box and activated the gifts and fruit of the Holy Spirit.

You might refer to the Scripture Encounter entitled Availability of the Holy Spirit and Appendix 'G'– Receiving The Holy Spirit – Baptism In The Holy Spirit.

– I AM AFRAID OF CHANGE – Page 30

I know my present life is incompatible with my emotional, spiritual and physical needs but I am afraid to change. It is easy for you to saying, *Just Try It!* or imply that it is just a simple decision but how do I get by this fear?

People who attend Inner Healing Workshops often come because they sense a need to change or feel a dissonance in their lives. Their Spirit senses a dissonance, and the dissonance causes confusion and unsettled feelings. We might for example feel that our present life is incompatible with our emotional needs. It is reasonable to be afraid of change.

Changing our lives is often difficult because of existing loyalties to family and friends. Loyalty to decisions we have made earlier in our life can also hold us back. Family structure, our community and our living situation might burden us and limit us. People might be sucking the strength out of our body, our mind, our soul and our spirit.

The problem is that once we are aware of the dissonance, we can't just cancel that awareness. We have to make choices. We realized in Section 5, 'The Separation of Body, Mind, Soul, and Spirit', that choices affect every area of our being. To be whole we need to allow the Holy Spirit to enter into each choice and guide us towards wholeness. If something or someone is sucking the strength out of our emotions, out of our body, soul or spirit we need to follow the Spirit's lead.

In the healing process we learn to detach ourselves from objects and people who draw strength from us. Healing demands action. Healing might mean leaving outmoded beliefs, behaviors, relationships and moving toward more healthy relationships. My brother Ron had a phrase, "choice predicates action." It is like in the John 5: 8-9 where it says *"Rise, take up your bed and walk."*

Q 6
It's all about relationship.

– IT'S ALL ABOUT RELATIONSHIP – Page 35

It seems to me that you are just trying to entrap people into using your system and hook them into you and your ideas. You keep say '*Five Fold Cycle* Works' and '*Just Try It! FFC Works…*'. Aren't you just like the other evangelists and people involved in Christian healing, just out to make money?

I am sorry if you have read this into my work. I am suggesting people use the system but not to make the system their god or focusing on it as a fix all. Rather my pastoral interest is in you forming a relationship with God; Father, Son and Holy Spirit. Healing comes from God and the *Five Fold Cycle* encourages and directs people to the triune God.

The first step is to open to God, which means to become personal with God and to join to Him like a branch to the tree. The second step is to meet the Holy Spirit, to listen to the Holy Spirit and to be interactive with the Holy Spirit. We do that, as we gain a relationship of attentiveness to the Spirit's soft and gentle voice and to the Spirit's direction: Word of Knowledge, Word of Wisdom and Gift of Discernment of Spirits. Connecting with the Spirit is another part of the relationship with God. The third and fourth steps encourage connection to Jesus. Step five focus back on God who is # 1. It's all about relationship – we were created for relationship.

God from all eternity has been seeking an intimate relationship with us. Knowing that there would be a Fall (Genesis 3: 1-24) and the Tower of Babel (Genesis 11: 1-9), God laid out a number of steps to bring us back to Him. He sent Jesus to clean us up and make us righteous so that we could come into His presence. He sent the Holy Spirit to reside in us and teach, comfort, heal and walk with us in every moment of the day. Through the Holy Spirit, the Father gave us Gifts. Courage and Fortitude are to strengthen us, Wisdom and Understanding are to help our minds be clear. Tongues is to heal the break from the Tower of Babel, bring languages together. Healing and Miracles are signs and wonders to encourage us. And there is much much more. The only thing that limits the Holy Spirit is you and me.

To recapitulate: *Five Fold Cycle – Method of Healing Personal H*urt is a method of helping people come to God, meet Him and receive His blessings – healing and wholeness. Incorporating these ideas into your daily life will change the way you deal with problems. Every problem will become an opportunity – a time to come closer to God. As you form this relationship to God, our Father and Creator, you will no longer need this book.

Q 7
Be Holy.

— BE HOLY - Page 39

It is way beyond my imagination to be able to live up to the phrase 'be holy as your Heavenly Father is holy'. This is a challenge beyond our capabilities. You said we are broken people. How do you expect us to meet this goal?

Being holy means, we live differently than others – set apart. 'Be perfect, therefore, as your heavenly Father is perfect' (Matthew 5: 48). Being set apart for God means that we live a life for God:

- We try to be holy in all we do, through the Holy Spirit.
- We look different than the world.
- We seek to live according to God's wisdom – God's Word.
- We imitate God rather than the ways of the world.
- His holy presence in our lives produces in us a loving obedience.

God has called you His own and set you apart and made you holy — different.

Here is a taste of what scripture says that confirms this position and calling by God:

> *But you are a chosen people, a royal priesthood, a holy nation, God's own people, in order that you may proclaim the excellence of him who called you out of darkness into his marvelous light.*
> 1 Peter 2: 9

> *[17] Therefore come out from them, and be separate from them, says the Lord, and touch nothing unclean; then I will welcome you, [18] and I will be your father, and you shall be my sons and daughters, says the Lord Almighty."*
> 2 Corinthians 6: 17-18

> *Do not be conformed to this age, but be transformed by the renewing of the mind, so that you may discern what is the will of God—what is good and acceptable and perfect.*
> Romans 12: 2

There is a calling on our life to be 'holy.' We as broken people reach out to God. Isaiah described our condition:

> *All of us have become like one who is unclean, and all our righteous acts are like filthy rags; we all shrivel up like a leaf, and like the wind our sins sweep us away.*
> Isaiah 64: 6

We know we are unclean, like filthy rags, and that our good works will never bring us holiness. It is the cleansing Blood of Jesus that brings us righteousness. This freely given grace with the help of the Holy Spirit, begins us to transformed and renewed.

Q 8
Why use the process?

– WHY USE THE PROCESS? – Page 44

We are told that no two healings are ever the same; therefore, prayer for healing can never be reduced to a formula or method. How can we then use the Method of Healing Personal Hurt – Five Fold Cycle?

Good question. Yes, it is true that no two healings are ever the same because each of us is an individual, unique person, and each of us relates to God, the Father, the Son and the Holy Spirit in an individual and unique manner. The Five Fold Cycle is a framework offering five steps but it does not control the interaction each of us has with our Creative God. Let me explain.

In the first step Five Fold Cycle directs us to come to God. The Method directs us to open to God and to join to him – abide in Him. How we open to God, whether we open to God, and how we experience 'abiding in Him' is not controlled or formulated in any way. This is an individual and unique experience that is permitted by our choice to 'open' to our Father God.

In step two we are directed to open to the Holy Spirit and listen to the Spirit's direction. Again, this is an individual experience. No two experiences will be the same as we are unique and wonderfully created individuals. The first step suggested a relationship with the Father. This step suggests a relationship with the Holy Spirit and an opening to His Gifts to understand and see into the roots of our life.

Next, we move to step three and four – the Cross of Jesus. Again, this is an opening to the individual and unique relationship each of has with Jesus and His transforming Love. You as an individual come to meet Jesus and He as the Son of God through His death and Resurrection takes our wounds and through the exchange on the Cross we obtain the blessing - Healing.

As you can see each step encourages the building of our 'relational healing.' We are opening a relationship with God as Father, Spirit and Son and gaining wholeness in ourselves and our identity. Finally, in step five, we move off ourselves and abide in Him.

Q 9	
Be specific!	**– BE SPECIFIC! – Page 48**

You said that in the problem-solving process it is necessary to be specific, why?

We all know that God can do anything. He is the creator and can re-create or diminish if he chooses. So where does this understanding come from, that we should be specific?

In scripture Jesus was very specific. He often asked the question 'what do you want of me?'

> *Then Jesus said to him, 'What do you want me to do for you?' The blind man said to him, 'My teacher, let me see again.'*
> Mark 10: 51

The same statement from Jesus is also found in Luke 18: 41 and Matthew 20: 32. Jesus did not work with generalities but specific requests. Individual people called out to Him, and he responded individually 'what can I do for you?'

In Healing Prayer, we ask what is the root cause, what is the specific issue? We are looking for the foundational experience and bringing that to the Cross where we seek healing through Jesus' death and resurrection.

Q 10	
Darkness to Light.	**– DARKNESS TO LIGHT – Page 57**

Why is there all this comparison of light and darkness? We are told in Ephesians 8 that we were children of darkness and need to become children of light. Explain the symbolism.

The comparison between darkness and light probably started with creation when God created the universe it says, "there was evening and then there was morning" (Genesis 1: 2-5). God takes us from darkness to light, from fear to peace, from confusion to understanding and sin to wholeness.

For our entire life we are moving away from darkness and moving closer to the Father of Lights (James 1: 17). To be Born Again (John 3: 3) means we pass through the barrier, the ripped curtain (Matthew 27: 50-51), become a new creation, (2 Corinthians 5: 17), we cross over, leaving one land and entering another. We are grafted into the Hebrew people, who crossed over the Red Sea and the Jordan River to enter a New Promised Land. We move away from the broken darkness of Egypt to the light of the Promised Land. Wonderful symbolism!

Lucifer is the Angel of Light who has fallen and is now Darkness. Christ now sits in glory. God the Father is described as light:

> *⁵ This is the message we have heard from him and proclaim to you, that God is light and in him there is no darkness at all.*
> 1 John 1: 5

Scripture invites us to choose righteousness – the light of dawn:

> *But the path of the righteous is like the light of dawn, which shines brighter and brighter until full day. The way of the wicked is like deep darkness; they do not know what they stumble over.*
> Proverbs 4: 18-19

We are on a journey from darkness, brokenness to healing with wholeness and light.

Q 11 – Using your imagination.

– USING YOUR IMAGINATION – Page 68

When we use our imagination aren't we just dreaming and fantasying? What value is it to pretend in that way?

In healing prayer, we often encourage people to envision the memory or ask the Holy Spirit to bring the event back to memory. Our imagination is a gift from the Lord and is very effective in healing of memories and inner healing prayer. We use our imagination as a tool, envisioning the Lord Jesus coming into the memory and watch as His presence touches the memory. We know that God is not caught up in time, place and space, therefore can easily go back in time with us. In fact, He was back in that time with us, but we often could not experience His presence.

Visions, dreams and imagination are often used by the Holy Spirit as a form of the Word of Knowledge and Word of Wisdom. With these Gifts we can bring back memories and envision them sometimes as a single frame and sometimes as full moving pictures with color, motion and sound.

The question we would often pose during healing prayer is "watch the Lord Jesus and see what he does in the memory."

In Appendix 'B' I share a story where I saw Jesus 'on the back of the bicycle I was driving. His hair just flowed out to the back as we sped along the street in Medicine Hat, Alberta.' After using my imagination in that prayer, my loneliness was gone.

Q 12 Inner Healing Prayer.

– INNER HEALING PRAYER - Page 83

How does this Healing of Memories or Inner Healing Prayer work? Could you explain the healing process and the action of Jesus Christ and His Holy Spirit?

To answer this question, I am going to quote Leanne Payne from her book *The Broken Images: Restoring Personal Wholeness Through Healing Prayer,* pages 27-28.*

> **"The Power of the Memory**
> In prayer for the healing of memories, the power of the memory to make the past present to us in a very real way is extraordinary. The reason for this, of course, is that Jesus, the Infinite One who is outside of time and to whom *all times are present,* enters into what for us is a past occurrence, one known only in retrospect, though we experience its consequences in the present. Here the past-present-future time sequence in which we experience existence comes together in a particularly meaningful way with the Eternal. And that which is eternal within us and therefore not bound by time is sparked. In this way we experience past and present as one—a foretaste perhaps of a way of knowing earth-time we shall one day experience when we are no longer bound by space, mass, and time.
>
> **The Holy Spirit's Action in the Healing of Memories**
> The *essential* action, that which differentiates healing of memories from psychological methodologies, is the action of the Holy Spirit pointing to *the Presence of our Lord who is there.* He has, as it were, walked into that darkest hell of our existence; and even in the midst of the unfolding memory drama, we look with the eyes of our heart (and as so often happens) are enabled to see Him. We receive from Him that healing word, glance, or embrace we've so long needed. We forgive others their darkest sins against us, and He forgives us our sins, and we receive from Him who manifests the very love of God the Father the healing grace we've been unable to receive before. We find out that He was there all along with that healing action, had we only been able to look up and receive it."

Through Inner Healing Prayer, the Holy Spirit moves quietly and powerfully to bring psychological wholeness, helping to integrate the Body, Mind, Soul and Spirit.

---

*Payne, Leanne. *The Broken Images: Restoring Personal Wholeness Through Healing Prayer*, Crossroads Books, Westchester, Illinois, 1981.

Q 13
Accepting Jesus in your heart.

– ACCEPTING JESUS IN YOUR HEART – Page 103

Why do we have to accept Jesus into our heart? There is nowhere in the Bible that has the Sinner's Prayer or Prayer for Salvation.

It might come as a surprise that nowhere does scripture specifically refer to 'praying to accept Jesus into your heart.' Instead, what scripture emphasizes is relationship – trust/faith in who Jesus is and what he has done through His death and resurrection.

We come to understand that faith is dynamic. It is more than agreeing to a formula. In the act or decision, we are beginning a transformation over time, opening our life to the Lord and His Spirit. The evidence of which is the Fruit of the Spirit in our lives.

www.ingramcontent.com/pod-product-compliance
Lightning Source LLC
Chambersburg PA
CBHW082209070526
44585CB00020B/2344